MODES
EXPLAINED

BY CARL CULPEPPER

To access video visit:
www.halleonard.com/mylibrary

Enter Code
2536-0365-1509-3722

ISBN 978-1-5400-6256-7

HAL•LEONARD®

Visit Hal Leonard Online at
www.halleonard.com

Contact us:
Hal Leonard
7777 West Bluemound Road
Milwaukee, WI 53213
Email: info@halleonard.com

In Europe, contact:
Hal Leonard Europe Limited
42 Wigmore Street
Marylebone, London, W1U 2RN
Email: info@halleonardeurope.com

In Australia, contact:
Hal Leonard Australia Pty. Ltd.
4 Lentara Court
Cheltenham, Victoria, 3192 Australia
Email: info@halleonard.com.au

CONTENTS

INTRODUCTION

The topic of modes has long been one of mystery and allure for many aspiring musicians, and this statement seems especially true of modern electric guitarists who seek to develop their improvisational skills. While a proper understanding of modal concepts is part and parcel to applied theory in contemporary music, the development of this knowledge can be elusive.

The scope of this book, along with the accompanying video, is to provide you with a multi-dimensional approach to understanding modes as applied to rock-related genres. A combination of theoretical principles and practical applications are presented in an effort to solidify your understanding of modes in such a way that will integrate with your overall musicality. This requires the theoretical and practical aspects to merge, ultimately resulting in an intuitive musical approach. Not only will the skills associated with improvisation improve dramatically, but your entire understanding of harmonic relationships in music will deepen.

While a prior study of the fundamentals in music theory would be beneficial to anyone using this book, the material is presented in such a way that it can be absorbed by motivated students with only the most basic skills. Be sure to look up the definitions to any unfamiliar musical terms that you might encounter. And, if needed, spend a little extra time studying any underlying musical concepts (i.e., chords, major scales, intervals, etc.) that could make learning easier.

The subject of modes is both simple in essence and complex in potential. With this in mind, it is crucial to seek first a basic understanding before pursuing the infinite possibilities and concepts. Give yourself time to develop. Many aspiring musicians make the mistake of assuming too much about their own knowledge of this subject. This commonly results in a halting of progress. Keep an open mind as you proceed and cultivate a habit of endeavoring further with whatever you think you already know. I guarantee that you will not "get to the bottom of it" with your study of modes (or music theory, in general). The possibilities are virtually endless, and this is what makes it fun! At the end of the day, it is my sincere hope that this book and video package will be both informative and enjoyable as you explore the topic of modes.

ABOUT THE VIDEO

Each solo has been filmed for your studies, featuring myself playing through each solo and breaking each concept down into the various building blocks discussed in each chapter. Each filmed segment is indicated by the ▶ icon placed next to a chapter or section heading. To access the video content, simply go to *www.halleonard.com/mylibrary* and input the unique code printed on the first page of this book.

A LITTLE BACKGROUND

Centuries ago, the methods of creating music did not include many of the elements of tonality that we now take for granted. It was during the early stages of establishing harmonic principles that the concept of modes as we know it began to appear. As music progressed into and through the Renaissance Period (approx. 1400–1600 CE), melodies were often composed with a static bass note (or drone). This is especially present in lute music. This constant tone serves to anchor the relationship of the melody to the keynote. As we will discover, this kind of static context creates the purest form of modal application.

Strictly modal music does not make use of many tonal elements like tension/release and chord progression. And, generally speaking, such was the case for most of the music before 1600. From about 1600 to 1900 (the common practice period for tonal music), most musicians and composers eschewed modal habits in favor of pursuing the blossoming system of tonal music. While elements of the modal approach were occasionally used within tonal music during this time, it was not the prevailing method.

At the onset of the 20th century, musicians and composers began looking for new ways to structure music, as the tonal system seemed to have peaked in the previous centuries. Some considered the possibility of discarding the entire concept of tonality in favor of daring new systems like serialism and microtonal music. However, a new universe of possibilities opened up with the marriage of tonal and modal concepts that sprung up in the popular music of the day. Spearheading this new movement were jazz musicians seeking to develop a vocabulary for improvising over complex tonal chord progressions. And it is this legacy from which we draw our inspiration.

MODAL MUSIC VS. TONAL MUSIC

- **Tonal music** utilizes tension and release in order to make the music "breathe" and move. Not only does this drive the melodic content, it is also the driving force behind chord progression.

- **Modal music** tends to be anchored to the keynote, often by the use of a pedal tone, drone, or a static chord. This allows the colors (interval qualities) present in the mode to be used freely.

With these basic parameters defined, it is easy to think that modal music is very simple. But it is this simplicity that creates an environment of possibilities. Add to that, the fact that a combination of tonal and modal concepts can be exponentially complex.

CHAPTER 1
MODES DEFINED ▶

MAJOR AND RELATIVE MINOR SCALES

Most musicians are familiar with the basic concept of modes without even knowing it. Often, the first modal situation music students encounter is that of the **relative minor**. When the notes of a major scale are reassigned with its sixth degree as the root, it produces a different mood. Compare the C major scale with its relative, A minor.

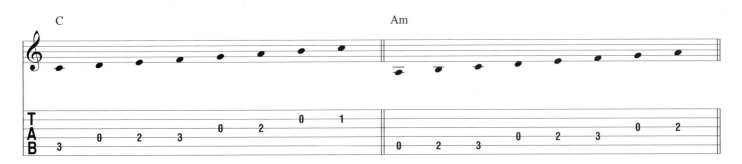

While the C major scale has a happy, uplifting sound, the A minor scale has a sad or dark mood. They share the same notes, so how can this be? By arranging the notes in a way that the A sounds like the root (or keynote), we now hear the notes based on their relationship to A, not C. The stepwise structure (order of half steps and whole steps) of the scale is now very different. It is easy to see this when we lay the scales out on one string.

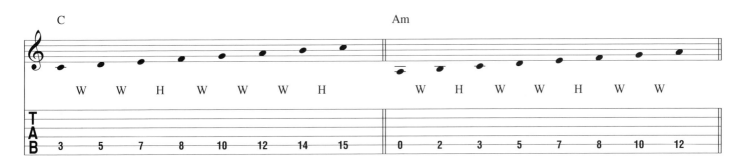

In the most basic terms, C major and A minor are the major and minor modes of the same group of notes. And because the structure is the formula for the scale, this relationship of the major and minor modes exists in all keys. The relative minor is always found on the sixth degree of the major key.

For the simple purpose of illustration, the scales are shown here in one octave, starting and stopping on the root note. But, within real music, other factors such as reiteration of a note within the phrasing and chords are important to the perception of a note as the root.

DERIVATIVE MODES OF THE MAJOR SCALE

While the major/relative minor relationship is a very substantial concept that is widely employed throughout the music of Western civilization, the major scale contains seven unique modes, one for each scale degree.

1. **Ionian** (same as the major scale): The root is the first degree of the major scale.
2. **Dorian:** The root is the second degree of the major scale.
3. **Phrygian:** The root is the third degree of the major scale.
4. **Lydian:** The root is the fourth degree of the major scale.
5. **Mixolydian:** The root is the fifth degree of the major scale.
6. **Aeolian** (same as the relative/natural minor scale): The root is the sixth degree of the major scale.
7. **Locrian:** The root is the seventh degree of the major scale.

Let's reimagine the notes of the C major scale arranged into each of the seven relative modes.

IONIAN

The first mode of the C major scale is C Ionian. The arrangement of whole steps (W) and half steps (H) is the same as the major scale: W–W–H–W–W–W–H.

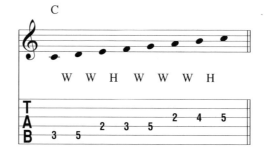

Take note of the "uplifting" mood of the Ionian scale. It is often used to convey a happy or positive emotion.

DORIAN

The second mode of the C major scale is D Dorian. The stepwise formula is: W–H–W–W–W–H–W.

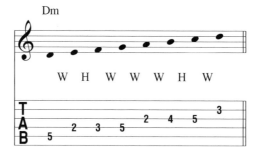

The mood of this mode is similar to the natural minor scale, but it is not quite as intensely dark or sad.

PHRYGIAN

The third mode of the C major scale is E Phrygian. Its stepwise formula is: H–W–W–W–H–W–W.

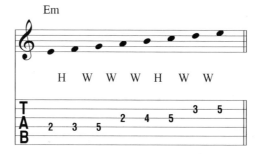

The mood of the Phrygian mode is even more intense than the natural minor scale. The tension in this mode makes it effective in conveying an aggressive feeling in the music.

LYDIAN

The fourth mode of the C major scale is F Lydian. Its stepwise formula is: W–W–W–H–W–W–H.

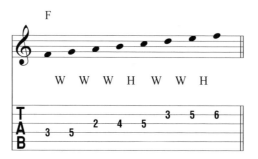

The Lydian mode has a lifted mood similar to the major scale. But unlike the major scale, it is a bit mysterious. It's often used to evoke feelings of expectation or adventure.

MIXOLYDIAN

The fifth mode of the C major scale is G Mixolydian. Its stepwise formula is: W–W–H–W–W–H–W.

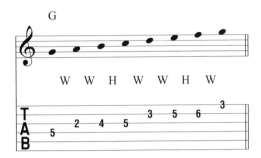

The Mixolydian mode has a similar mood to that of the major scale, but it is not quite as "happy" sounding.

AEOLIAN

The sixth mode of the C major scale is A Aeolian. The stepwise formula is the same as natural minor: W–H–W–W–H–W–W.

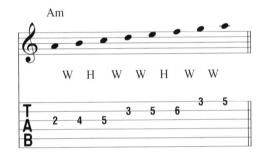

Since they are basically synonymous, Aeolian has the same dark mood as that of the minor scale. It can convey a very serious, sad emotion.

LOCRIAN

The seventh mode of the C major scale is B Locrian. Its stepwise formula is: H–W–W–H–W–W–W.

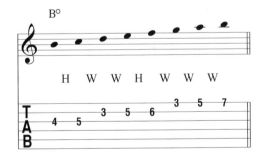

The Locrian mode is loaded with tension, which makes it feel very unstable.

By reassigning the root to each note of the same major scale, we are able to derive these seven unique modes. This derivative approach shows us that the notes belonging to one major key are capable of producing a variety of musical moods. From a guitarist's viewpoint, it is important to realize that any major scale pattern can be used for any of its seven modes.

Remember: Modes are not fretboard positions, nor do they require patterns that start on any particular note of the key. Modes are defined by application.

PARALLEL METHOD FOR MODES

The derivative method described in the previous section shows how the major scale contains a variety of moods present in its modes. It also illustrates the shared notes between a mode and its relative major scale. However, the sound of each mode is a result of its unique interval structure. For this reason, it is important to comprehend the scale formulas that come from comparing modes to their parallel (i.e. from the same root note) major scales.

IONIAN

Since the Ionian scale starts on the first degree of the major scale, it shares the same stepwise formula (W–W–H–W–W–W–H). And the degrees are numbered the same: 1, 2, 3, 4, 5, 6, and 7.

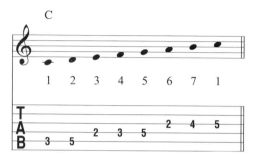

The mood is unaltered from that of the major scale. The basic chord built on the root (the "I" chord) is a major triad (1, 3, 5). Therefore, Ionian is one of the three major modes of the major scale. Ionian is commonly played over major and major 7th chords.

DORIAN

When compared to the parallel major scale, the stepwise formula for the Dorian mode (W–H–W–W–W–H–W) yields the following set of degrees: 1, 2, ♭3, 4, 5, 6, and ♭7.

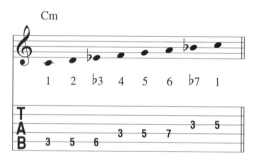

The "I" chord in Dorian is a minor triad (1, ♭3, 5). Therefore, Dorian is one of the three minor modes of the major scale. Compare the Dorian mode to its parallel minor, as well. The ♮6 degree is what makes it different from a minor scale (which has a ♭6). The Dorian mode is commonly played over minor 6th, minor 7th, minor 9, minor 11, and minor 13 chords.

PHRYGIAN

When compared to the parallel major scale, the stepwise formula for the Phrygian mode (H–W–W–W–H–W–W) yields the following set of degrees: 1, ♭2, ♭3, 4, 5, ♭6, and ♭7.

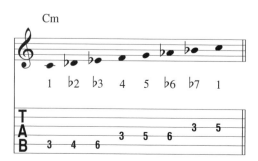

The "I" chord in Phrygian is a minor triad (1, ♭3, 5). Therefore, Phrygian is one of the three minor modes of the major scale. The ♭2 degree is what makes it different from the natural minor scale (which has a ♮2 degree). It can be played over a minor chord.

LYDIAN

When compared to the parallel major scale, the stepwise formula for the Lydian mode (W–W–W–H–W–W–H) yields the following set of degrees: 1, 2, 3, #4, 5, 6, and 7.

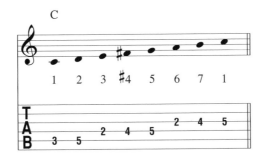

The "I" chord in Lydian is a major triad (1, 3, 5). Therefore, Lydian is one of the three major modes. The #4 degree makes it different from a major scale. Lydian is commonly played over major 7th and major 7#11 chords.

MIXOLYDIAN

When compared to the parallel major scale, the stepwise formula for the Mixolydian mode (W–W–H–W–W–H–W) yields the following set of degrees: 1, 2, 3, 4, 5, 6, and ♭7.

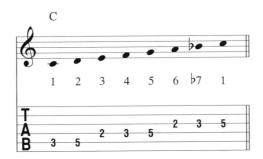

The "I" chord in Mixolydian is a major triad (1, 3, 5). Therefore, Mixolydian is one of the three major modes. The ♭7 degree makes it different from a major scale. Mixolydian is commonly played over major and dominant 7th chords.

AEOLIAN

When compared to the parallel major scale, the stepwise formula for the Aeolian mode (W–H–W–W–H–W–W) yields the following set of degrees: 1, 2, ♭3, 4, 5, ♭6, and ♭7. This formula is the same as the natural minor scale.

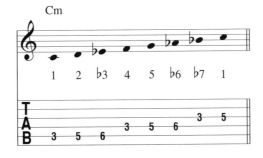

The "I" chord in Aeolian is a minor triad (1, ♭3, 5). Therefore, Aeolian is one of the three minor modes of the major scale. Since the formula is same as the natural minor scale, it has the same mood. Aeolian is commonly played over a minor chord.

LOCRIAN

When compared to the parallel major scale, the stepwise formula for the Locrian mode (H–W–W–H–W–W–W) yields the following set of degrees: 1, ♭2, ♭3, 4, ♭5, ♭6, and ♭7.

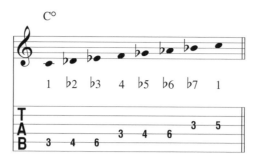

The "I" chord in Locrian is a diminished triad (1, ♭3, ♭5). This makes it unique among the major scale modes. The absence of a legitimate tonic triad (musically resolved, like a major or minor chord) contributes to the highly unstable nature of the Locrian mode. It is usually played over a diminished triad or minor 7♭5 chord.

COMBINE THE DERIVATIVE AND PARALLEL METHODS FOR DEEPER UNDERSTANDING

Both the derivative and parallel methods for defining modes are effective for arriving at the correct notes. But it is only through the merging of the two perspectives that you will begin to fully comprehend the modal concept. Consider the following examples:

- Find C Locrian by applying the Locrian formula (1, ♭2, ♭3, 4, ♭5, ♭6, ♭7) to C. See that this is the seventh mode of D♭ major.
- Find D Lydian by applying the Lydian formula (1, 2, 3, ♯4, 5, 6, 7) to D. See that this is the fourth mode of A major.
- Find G Phrygian by applying the Phrygian formula (1, ♭2, ♭3, 4, 5, ♭6, ♭7) to G. See that this is the third mode of E♭ major.

Repeat this process with each mode, starting on every possible note.

STEP AWAY FROM THE GUITAR!

It's good practice to work this information out on paper; you can write out the notes for various modes by name just as above. It isn't necessary to use music notation (although, that's even better). By putting the guitar down for a bit, you will allow yourself to formulate a pure approach without the distractions (and temptations) of guitar techniques and fretboard visualization. It is important to separate these steps of study.

PICK UP THE GUITAR

Once you feel comfortable with the basic information, try finding the notes for any mode on the guitar fretboard. The applied examples in the following chapters (and videos) are presented in a manner that will help you connect the abstract concept of modes to the practical techniques of guitar soloing. Go at your own pace and feel free to bounce around the chapters as you please.

APPLYING THESE CONCEPTS TO OTHER SCALES

In this study, we will be primarily concerned with applying these methods to the modes of the major scale. But it is important to realize that any unique scale has its own set of modes. For instance, the harmonic minor scale has a stepwise formula that differs from that of the major/relative minor scale: W–H–W–W–H–W+H–H, with the degrees being the root, 2, ♭3, 4, 5, ♭6, and 7. Therefore, it has its own unique set of modes (see Appendix). Likewise, the melodic minor scale has its own unique stepwise formula: W–H–W–W–W–W–H, with the degrees being the root, 2, ♭3, 4, 5, 6, and 7.

After becoming familiar and comfortable with the modes of the major scale, I encourage you to apply the derivative and parallel methods to the harmonic minor and melodic minor scales, in particular. This will open up a whole new world of melodic and harmonic possibilities.

Pro tip: A thorough understanding of the melodic minor modes is crucial to the study of modern jazz and jazz-fusion.

CHAPTER 2
IONIAN MODE SOLOING

IONIAN REVIEW

- Ionian is the first mode of the major scale. This is the familiar "do, re, mi, fa, sol, la, ti, do" scale.
- The stepwise formula for Ionian is: W–W–H–W–W–W–H.
- When compared to its parallel major scale, the degrees are numbered the same: 1, 2, 3, 4, 5, 6, 7.
- The "I" chord (or tonic) is a major triad or major 7th chord.
- The primary tension tone is the fourth degree, which tends to move down a half step to the major 3rd of the scale. The seventh degree can also have the tendency to lead up to the next root note.

MAJOR KEY TONALITY VS. IONIAN MODE

Tonal music uses the tension and release of the scale's interval structure to create motion in melodies and chord progressions. In contrast, modal music utilizes the variety of colors in the scale (including those tendency tones) in a more static context. For example, a bassist might be repeatedly playing (droning) a C note for an extended period of time while a guitarist is improvising over it with the C major scale (C Ionian). By remaining on the static C note, the bass note creates a static reference for the all the colors in the C scale of the solo.

The C major scale is the same as the C Ionian scale.

C Major/Ionian Scale   C Major/Ionian Scale Pattern (7th Position)

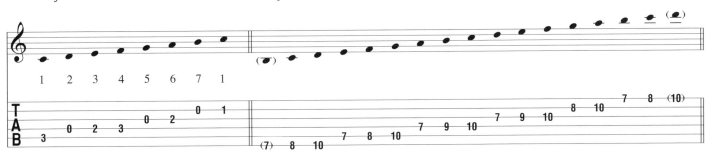

Since the degrees of the Ionian scale are the same as those in the major scale, any patterns that you know for the major scale will be applicable to Ionian-mode soloing.

SOLOING OVER A STATIC VAMP ▶

STUDY PREP

The example solo for this chapter was played over the following rhythm figure.

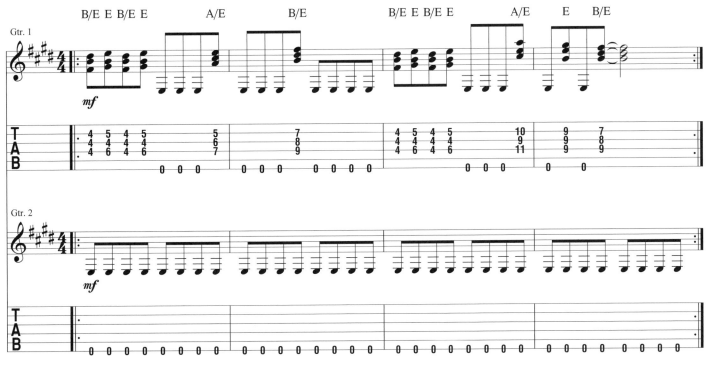

All of the notes in this riff are from E Ionian. The repeating E bass note (called a **pedal tone**) keeps the music anchored to the root. And while the riff contains a series of chords, the quick succession creates an impression of modal harmony against the E note rather than that of a tonal chord progression.

SCALE PATTERNS

In order to prepare for the examples in this chapter, make sure you are familiar with the E Ionian scale in the ninth and 11th positions.

E Ionian Scale (9th Position)

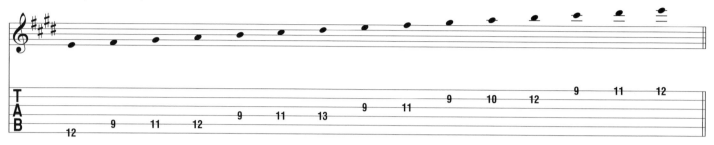

E Ionian Scale (11th Position, Three Notes Per String)

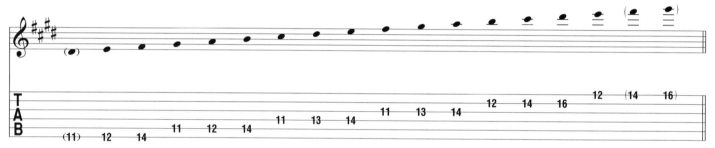

SOLO

Lick #1

Moderate Rock ♩ = 126

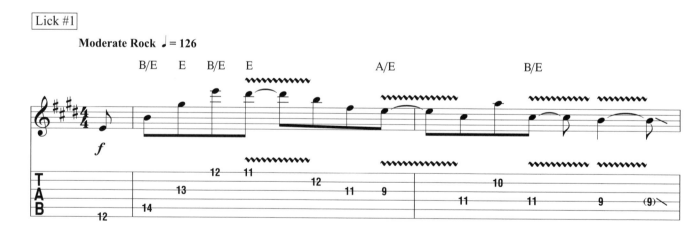

Lick #2

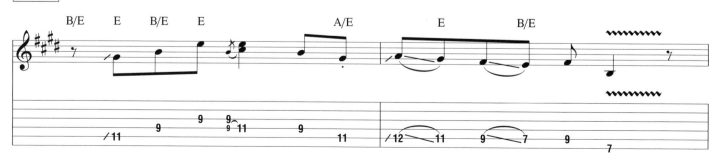

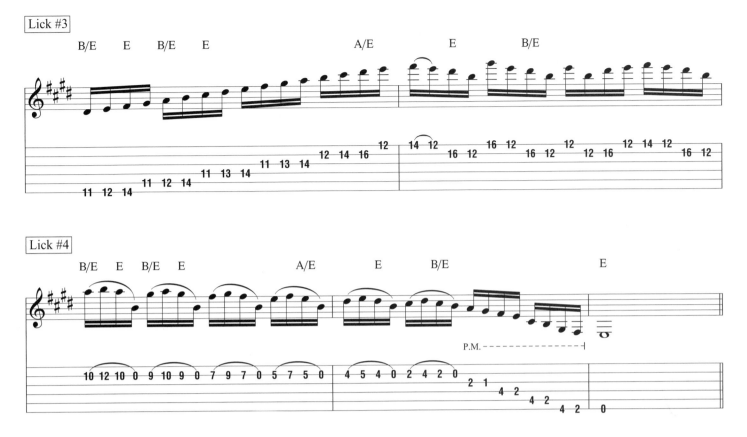

LICK #1

The first lick in the solo is comprised of the three major triad arpeggios from E major. The E major arpeggio (E–G#–B) in the first measure is in an **open voicing**.

Ascending from the pickup note, the root (E) is followed by the 5th (B), the higher octave 3rd (G#) and high root (E). By skipping every other note, the arpeggio is "opened" up to a wider sound. The colorful major 7th (D#) in the middle of the first measure leads down to a B major arpeggio (B–D#–F#). This blends with the sound of the riff for a combined impression of an Emaj9 chord (E–G#–B–D#–F#). The notes of the A major triad (A–C#–E) lead into the next measure, ending on the 5th (B) of the key.

LICK #2

It is important to recognize the presence of the pentatonic scales within the modes of the major scale. Lick #2 starts its phrasing in the ninth position of the E major pentatonic scale (E–F#–G#–B–C#).

On the downbeat of measure 2, a slide up to the fourth degree (A) adds a bit of extra color to the otherwise pentatonic phrasing. Notice that this coincides with the A/E chord in the accompaniment.

LICK #3

The first half of Lick #3 is a simple 11th position scale run starting on the major 7th (D#). The line develops into a two-note per string sequence in the next measure. This repetitive set of tones outlines an Emaj9 chord (E–G#–B–D#–F#). Notice the changing high notes (F# and G#).

LICK #4

The legato sequence that initiates Lick #4 follows the E Ionian scale down the second string. By first becoming familiar with the stepwise pattern of the major scale along a single string, each segment of the line is easily visualized. Make sure to keep the hammer-ons and pull-offs evenly subdivided in 16th-note rhythms. The final descending two-note per string line transitions into an E major pentatonic scale.

FURTHER EXPLORATION OF THE IONIAN MODE

After taking time to work through the examples in this chapter, be sure to apply the concepts presented in your own improvisations and compositions. The tension tones (fourth and seventh degrees) of the Ionian mode can seem tricky to incorporate at times. But, with experimentation, you will develop an understanding of the colors they provide in the Ionian modal context. As your comfort level increases, you will find that your Ionian mode concepts and vocabulary will also be applicable whenever soloing over major and major 7th chords within regular chord progressions. The ideas are simply used for however long the chord is played in the progression.

CHAPTER 3
DORIAN MODE SOLOING

DORIAN REVIEW

- Dorian is the second mode of the major scale.
- The stepwise formula for Dorian is: W–H–W–W–W–H–W.
- When compared to its parallel major scale, the degrees for the Dorian mode are: 1, 2, ♭3, 4, 5, 6, and ♭7.
- The "I" chord (or tonic) in Dorian is a minor triad or minor 7th chord.
- There are no tension tones in Dorian. The strongest color tone is the ♮6.

Dorian is one of the three minor modes indigenous to the major scale. Using the key of G, let's compare it to the parallel major. Notice where the flatted third and seventh degrees have altered the pattern.

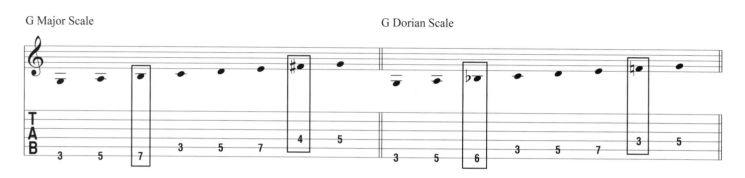

Now, compare G Dorian to G minor (Aeolian mode).

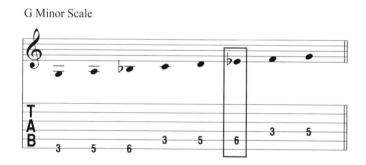

Play through the scales and notice how the ♮6 degree changes the mood of the Dorian from the darker sound of the pure minor scale.

TAKING ADVANTAGE OF PARALLEL AND DERIVATIVE THINKING FOR DORIAN

Since Dorian is the second mode of the major scale, the patterns for G Dorian will be the same as those for F major. The derivative method can help you to find your way around in Dorian if you know your major scale patterns. Just play the major scale that is a whole step down from the Dorian root. Once you do this, make sure to relate the scale to the Dorian root in order to understand its sound.

SOLOING OVER A STATIC VAMP ▶

STUDY PREP

The examples for this section were played over the following G Dorian riff in the accompanying video.

This riff is strictly composed from the Dorian scale, and it has no feeling of progression. Notice how the partial Gm13 chord emphasizes the ♮6 (E). Since the Dorian mode has no tension or tendency tones, you can experiment freely with the notes over this groove.

In preparation for the licks in this lesson, familiarize yourself with the third and tenth positions of the G Dorian scale.

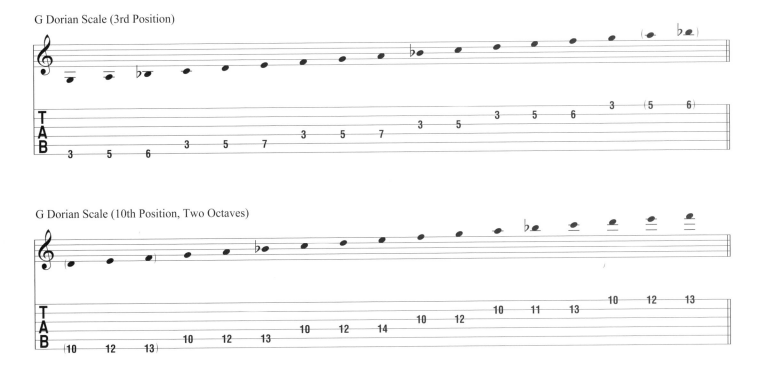

SOLO #1

Moderate Funk Rock ♩ = 96 (♪♪ = ♪♪³)

Lick #1

Gm13

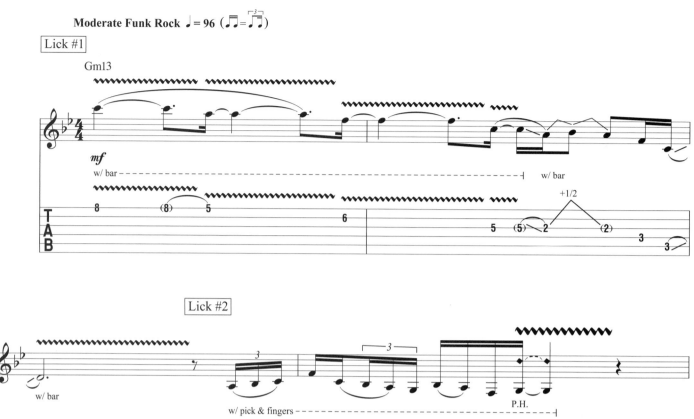

Lick #2

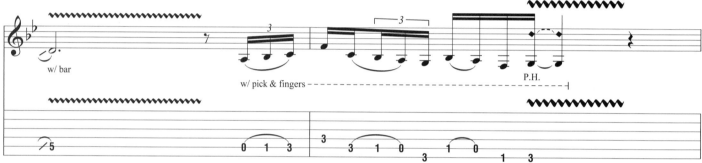

Lick #3

Lick #4

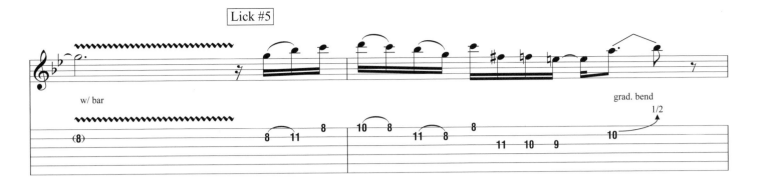

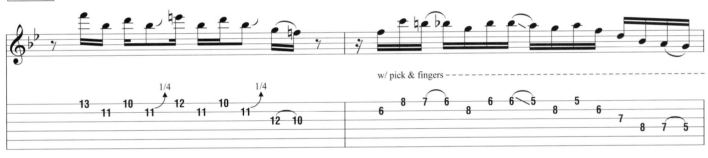

LICK #1

The arpeggios and chords present within a mode can be used melodically to accentuate its various colors. Notice how the F major triad (F–A–C) is used in Lick #1, highlighting the sounds of the second and fourth degrees. When we hear them as extensions of the chord like this, they are usually referred to by their compound interval names: the 9th and the 11th, respectively.

The liberal, but controlled, use of the whammy bar bestows a level of importance to each note. Pull up on the bar for the bend up to the minor 3rd (Bb) in measure 2. If you play this phrase on a guitar without a floating tremolo setup, then simply use finger vibrato and bending.

LICK #2

In Lick #2, the slurs and 16th-note triplets accentuate a scalar line centered around the notes of Gm7 (G–B♭–D–F). When playing this lick over the shuffle groove as demonstrated, take care with the timing. Going from the triplets to the 16th notes should feel quite natural within this shuffle feel context.

LICK #3

The third phrase starts with a Billy Gibbons-style trick, using a minor 3rd interval. First, slide into the third string, seventh fret (D) with the second finger. While continuing to hold down the third-string note, pluck the second-string F. Quickly mute the F, allowing the lower-string note (which is still being held) to ring out. Repeat this process as notated. The notes in parentheses are not struck but are simply allowed to ring out. Use the middle finger of the picking hand to pluck the second-string notes for a more percussive sound.

Appropriately, the lick ends with a shift down to the third position for a G minor pentatonic (G–B♭–C–D–F) phrase. The minor pentatonic scale makes a safe home base when playing on any of the diatonic minor modes.

LICK #4

In most modern situations, the blues scale can be used to add some style and extra chromatic color to the Dorian mode. The third-position G blues scale is utilized for the pull-offs in Lick #4. Again, the middle finger is used to give the higher string (this time, the third string) a bit of "snap." Notice that the lick is repetitive in nature, with a changing high note along the third string.

The phrase ends with a series of slurs on the third string, incorporating the second degree (A). Always take care to be accurate with half-step bends like the one found near the end. A quick slide up to the high G on the second string punctuates the line.

LICK #5

Although the short line in Lick #5 starts with another G minor pentatonic phrase, the focal point here is the descending chromaticism that targets the major 6th. Notice how the tritone interval between the C and the F♯ makes a strong impression before descending the scale to the G Dorian color tone (E). A slow half-step bend from A up to B♭ ends the lick.

LICK #6

The string skipping phrase at the beginning of Lick #6 makes prominent use of the Dorian color tone (major 6th). E is the low note of the pivot, as well as the high target note.

The second half of the lick is a little John Coltrane-inspired sequence. The G melodic minor scale (G–A–B♭–C–D–E–F♯) is evoked by starting on the accented major 7th (F♯). The sequence is based on a series of intervals of a 3rd: F♯–A, G–B♭, and A–C. Notice how the lower neighbor tones precede each interval on the way up.

About the use of melodic minor in Dorian mode: References to the melodic minor scale in this book are to that of the ascending mode* of the scale (root, 2, ♭3, 4, 5, 6, 7, octave root), regardless of the phrasing. Since the major 7th degree is the only differing note, the melodic minor scale is a great tool for introducing a bit of jazz phrasing to rock and blues in a Dorian context.

LICK #7

Lick #7 starts with a syncopated blues pivot lick. The slight bends on the ♭3 (B♭) bring out the blues style. Be careful not to bend too far; it's easy to accidentally make this note sound like the major 3rd (B). By alternating between the ♭7 (F) and the ♮6 (E), the Dorian color is emphasized.

The second half of the phrase incorporates the G Bebop Dorian scale (G–A–B♭–B–C–D–E–F–G). The addition of the major 3rd (B) as a passing tone produces musical tension when moving down the scale to the minor 3rd (B♭). The line ends with a descending B♭maj7 arpeggio (B♭–D–F–A). When played in the context of the G root, it combines for a Gm9 (G–B♭–D–F–A) sound.

---

*In the classical/traditional use of the melodic minor scale, the scale has both ascending and descending modes. The seventh and sixth degrees are typically flatted when descending melodies are played. The descending mode formula is: 1 (8va)–♭7–♭6–5–4–♭3–2–1.

LICK #8

The three major triads present in G Dorian (B♭, C, and F) are used in the first half of Lick #8. The high note is accented at the start of each three-note group, creating a syncopated pulse within the steady 16th-note rhythm.

The lick ends with an ascending two-note per string sequence. The highest note of each segment lands on the down beat, so be careful to stay in time. You can find a pattern of notes on the 15th and 17th fret of every string in this position. This consistent arrangement of notes is maintained until the second string, where the slide to the ♭7 is added before the punctuation of the line with the two high-G notes.

FURTHER EXPLORATION OF THE DORIAN MODE

For many, Dorian is the best place to start the journey of understanding modes. The absence of tension tones (sometimes referred to as **avoid notes**) makes it a context that can be explored without the fear of landing on a scale tone that sounds "wrong."

As your comfort level increases, you will find that your Dorian vocabulary will also be applicable whenever soloing over minor and minor 7th chords within regular chord progressions. The Dorian mode can often be applied in blues and blues-rock, wherever the minor pentatonic and blues scales work.

In the next section of this chapter, we will take a look at how to solo over a series of chords from the Dorian mode.

SOLOING OVER THE I–♭III–♭VII–IV PROGRESSION ▶

STUDY PREP

The examples for this section were played over the following E Dorian rhythm figure in the accompanying video.

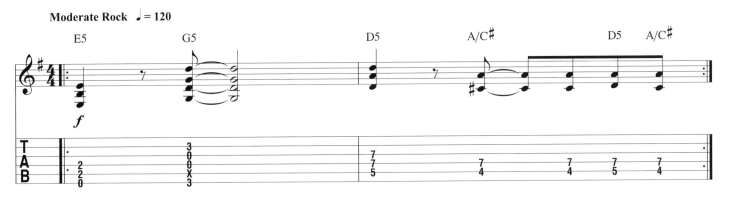

All the notes of the chords are from the E Dorian mode (E–F♯–G–A–B–C♯–D). In preparation for learning the licks from the sample solo, familiarize yourself with the following patterns for the E Dorian scale.

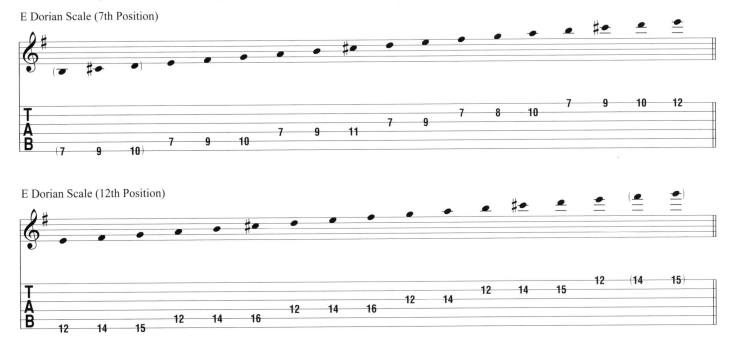

The alternate 12th-position pattern below utilizes a shift back to the 11th fret on the third and fourth strings in order to avoid the reaches on the fourth and fifth strings in the previous pattern.

E Dorian Scale (12th Position, Alternate Pattern)

These patterns will make a good starting point for learning the licks in the next section.

SOLO #2

Moderately Fast Rock ♩ = 120

*Bent note only.

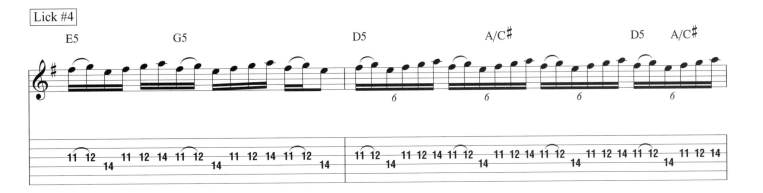

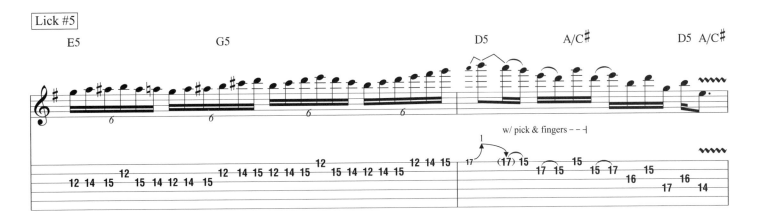

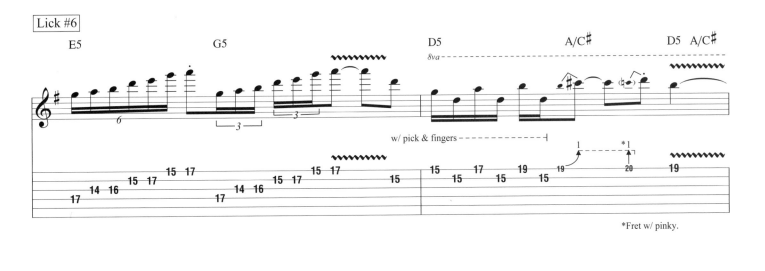

*Fret w/ pinky.

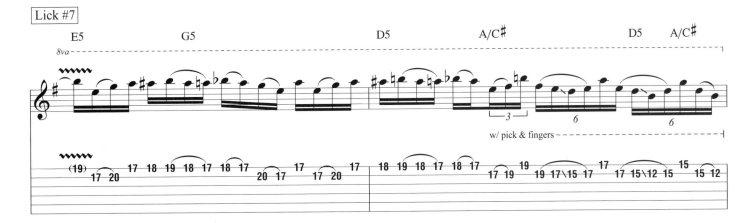

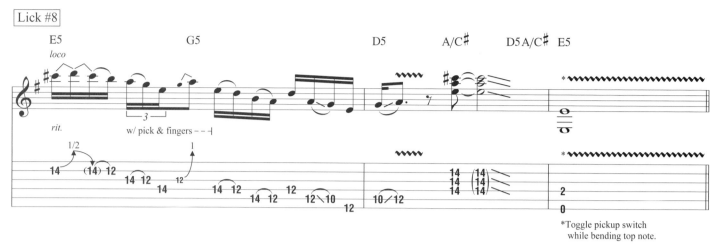

Lick #8

*Toggle pickup switch
while bending top note.

LICK #1

The first lick of the sample solo traces the chords of the riff underneath. Sliding into the 14th-fret B, the tonic chord is outlined with a simple ascending triad at the 12th position. The G, D, and A chords are all punctuated with a single triad shape moved along the top three strings. In each case, the note on the second string is bent up to the chord's major 3rd from a whole step below.

LICK #2

A three-note pickup starts Lick #2 in the second bar of the solo. The partial arpeggiation of Em7 (E–G–B–D) leads up to the half-step bending phrase on the downbeat. By using the scale's second degree, a bit of color is added to the otherwise minor pentatonic content. A simple E minor pentatonic (E–G–A–B–D) line ending on the root brings the phrase to a close.

LICK #3

The linear phrase in Lick #3 makes use of the E Blues scale (E–G–A♮–A♯–B–D). The odd-numbered grouping of the initial sequences gives the line an interesting rhythmic start. Notice the similarity in the articulation between the first five-note group and the next. The second half of the line is very straightforward in its ascending/descending scale run. Ending on the ♭3 (G) of the key, the line's resolution relates to the overall context of E Dorian rather than to the D5 and A/C♯ chords at that particular moment.

LICK #4

Lick #4 is derived from an Eddie Van Halen-style repetitive phrase. The second degree (F♯) adds color to the lick at the start of each six-note group. In the first bar, these groups are played in 16th-note timing, resulting in syncopated accents. Notice that the lick begins on beat 1, the "and" of beat 2, and then an abbreviated segment occurs on beat 4.

The second bar of the lick features the same phrase played in 16th-note triplets. At this point, the number of notes in each sequence correlates to the number of notes in each beat.

LICK #5

Lick #5 carries the 16th-note triplet momentum from the previous phrase into a Paul Gilbert-inspired picking sequence. The pattern played on the G and B strings of the first two beats is simply repeated on the B and E strings in the last two beats. The underlying scale shape is the result of adding the tritone (A♯) from the blues scale into the E Dorian scale.

The second half of the lick is based on the Em7 arpeggio. By using the fourth degree (A) to bend up to the 5th (B), a hint of pentatonic color is added into the chord tones. A simple skipping sequence is applied to the Em7 arpeggio pattern starting with the 15th-fret high G on the "and" of beat 2.

LICK #6

The first bar of Lick #6 features a pair of quick ascending E minor pentatonic scale runs. Notice that the second scale run starts on the "and" of beat 2, lending a bit of syncopation to the phrase.

An ascending scale fragment on the first string pivots off the second string D in the second half of Lick #6. The pivot note (D) ties the line to the underlying D5 chord at this point. The bend up to C♯ then correlates with the A/C♯ chord. While holding the bend to C♯, finger the 20th fret for the high D that follows. Here, the pitch of the note is one whole step higher than the normal fretted note, since the string is still bent. The phrase ends with a partial resolve to the fifth degree (B).

LICK #7

The E blues scale is utilized for the two-string phrasing that starts Lick #7. The first segment of the line is 12 notes long. Starting with the root (E) on the second 16th note of beat 1, it extends to the A note on beat 4. Notice that the phrase starts again with the E on the second 16th note of beat 4. This time, the phrase is cut short at the "and" of beat 2.

The Marty Friedman-style descending sequence that ends this lick is based on a series of pentatonic-derived segments. Beginning on the "and" of beat 2, the first segment incorporates the second degree (F#). The third finger is then barred across the 19th fret of the first string for the high B. This concept is then moved down to the appropriate fingerings for each of the next segments to end the line.

The five-note segments of this line create an interesting rhythmic effect when played in 16th-note triplet (six notes per beat) subdivisions. The result is a bit like the "falling down the stairs and landing on your feet" analogy. And be sure to stick the landing!

LICK #8

Initiating Lick #8, the sixth degree (C#) is used for the bend up to D and back. By prominently featuring the sixth degree against the underlying E5, the Dorian mood of the harmony is accentuated. The E minor pentatonic is used for the descending phrase that follows. Notice that the phrasing is based on descending groups of four.

The end of the lick features a series of a chord resolutions. The D5 chord on beat 1 is addressed by the slide from G up to A (the 5th of the chord). The A/C# chord is then practically doubled by the 14th-fret A triad (A–C#–E) in the solo. The lick (and solo) ends with the strong resolution of the octave root (E) in the last bar.

FURTHER EXPLORATION OF SOLOING OVER CHORDS FROM DORIAN

The example solo from this section represents only one of many possibilities of chord progressions derived from the Dorian mode. As you encounter more situations, be sure to balance the need for addressing the chords that are present with the freedom to express freely from the overall mode. Due to its lack of inherent tension, Dorian can be the most forgiving of modes with regards to using any of the notes at any time. However, musically strong phrasing often depends on a sense of connection between the melodic content (like a guitar solo) and the accompaniment (the rhythm section). Bottom line: keep the chords in mind.

CHAPTER 4
PHRYGIAN MODE SOLOING ▶

PHRYGIAN REVIEW

- Phrygian is the third mode of the major scale.
- The stepwise formula for Phrygian is: H–W–W–W–H–W–W.
- When compared to its parallel (from the same root) major scale, the degrees of Phrygian are: 1, ♭2, ♭3, 4, 5, ♭6, and ♭7.
- The "I" chord (or tonic) in Phrygian is a minor triad or minor 7th chord.
- The ♭2 and ♭6 degrees of the Phrygian scale create tension. The ♭2 sets it apart from the other two minor modes (Dorian and Aeolian).

Phrygian is one of the three minor modes indigenous to the major scale. The third mode of a C major scale would be E Phrygian.

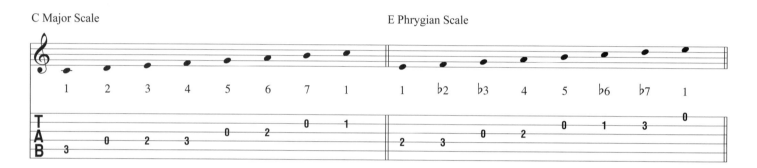

Now, compare E Phrygian to E major in order to realize the formula of 1, ♭2, ♭3, 4, 5, ♭6, and ♭7.

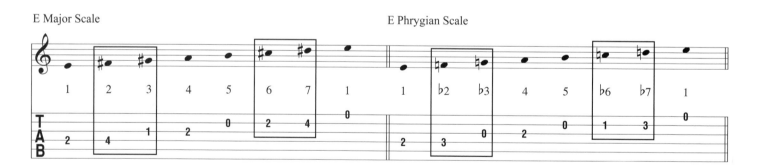

And notice how the ♭2 of Phrygian intensifies the mood when compared to the natural minor (Aeolian) scale.

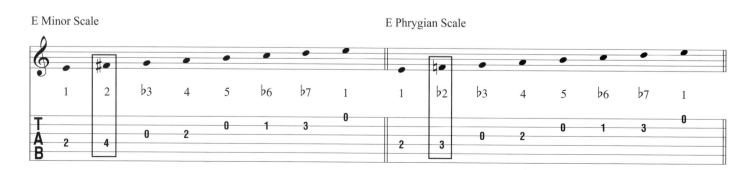

Since the E Phrygian scale shares its notes with C major, any patterns you know for the C major scale are applicable to the E Phrygian mode.

PHRYGIAN SOLO OVER A STATIC VAMP
STUDY PREP
The example solo for this section was played over the following rhythm figure:

All the notes of this riff reside within the F♯ Phrygian mode (F♯–G–A–B–C♯–D–E).

SCALE PATTERNS

Familiarize yourself with the following scale patterns for F♯ Phrygian in preparation for learning the licks from the example solo.

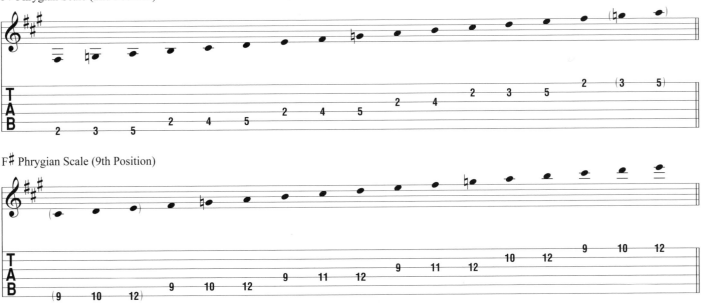

Since F♯ Phrygian is the third mode of D major, any scale patterns you know for the D major scale will be applicable to the F♯ Phrygian mode.

SOLO

Moderate Rock ♩ = 85 (♫ = ♫³)

Lick #1

F#7♭9(no3rd)

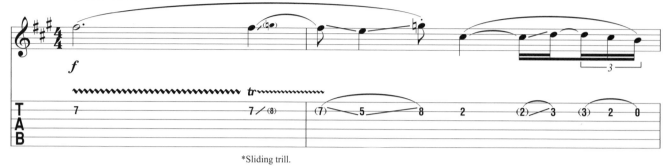

*Sliding trill.

Lick #2

Lick #3

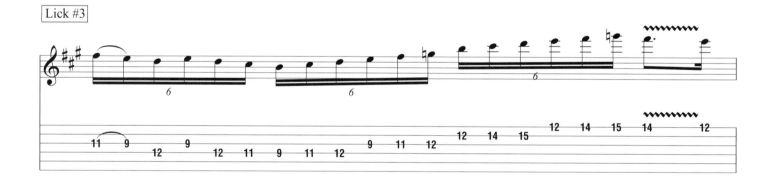

Lick #4   Lick #5

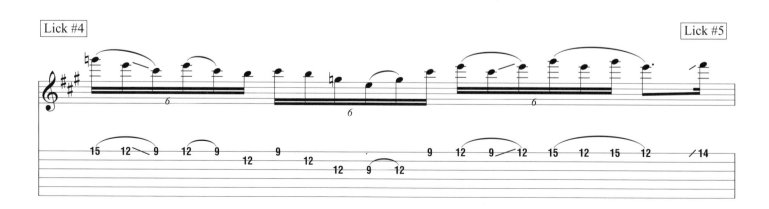

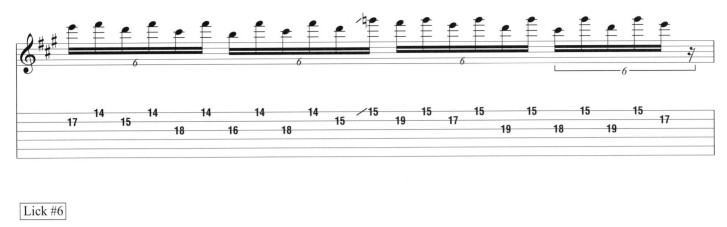

Lick #6

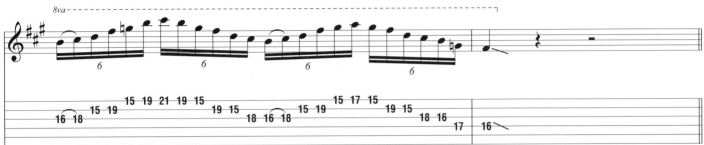

LICK #1

The single-string phrase in Lick #1 of the example solo uses slides to evoke a hint of Middle Eastern style. The trill at the end of the first measure is performed by rapidly sliding across the seventh and eighth frets. The ♭2 (G) in this trill immediately addresses the Phrygian sound. Notice how the line is generally centered around the F♯–C♯–E notes that fit the F♯7♭9(no 3rd) in the riff. The G, D, and B are used as auxiliary notes, adding color and tension to the phrase.

LICK #2

Another single-string phrase is played in Lick #2, but this time, it's played along the fourth string. The sequence is based on a series of three-note groups. Pick once and slur the rest of the line with hammer-ons, pull-offs, and slides as indicated. Since these three-note groupings are played in 16th-note rhythms (four notes per beat), the timing is syncopated. The shuffle feel of the groove adds an extra element of interest. Take care to stay in time!

LICK #3

The linear, 16th-note triplets in Lick #3 are played along a three-note per string pattern. Notice that by omitting the ♭3 (A), the pattern creates a repeating whole-step/half-step arrangement on each string.

A pair of descending three-note groups starts the line on beat 1 of the first measure. A steady ascent of the pattern begins with the fourth-string, ninth-fret B on beat 2. Again, the high G emphasizes the Phrygian mood just before resolving to the root (F♯) on beat 4.

LICK #4

The minor 7♭5 arpeggio (or chord) resides on the fifth degree within the Phrygian mode. This utilizes the ♭2, 4, 5, and ♭7 degrees of the mode.

The C♯m7♭5 arpeggio is sequenced in groups of three in Lick #4. Starting with the 15th-fret G, the first group of three notes is played by pulling off to the 12th fret and then sliding down to the ninth. Another pair of three-note groups lead down to the ninth-fret E. Notice that the second-string B is omitted in the second half of the lick, reducing the harmony to that of a C♯° triad (C♯–E–G).

LICK #5

The pivot lick in the next phrase is reminiscent of the neo-classical stylings of guitarists like Yngwie Malmsteen and Vinnie Moore. The first half of the phrase pivots from the F♯ on the first string, 14th fret with the scalar line descending the second and third strings. The second half of the phrase follows in the same manner, this time pivoting from the G at the 15th fret.

Take care with the timing, as this line is played in 16th-note triplets in spite of the intuitive two-note groupings. This type of lick is often played with upstrokes on the high notes and downstrokes on the lower notes. However, I prefer to use the middle finger of the picking hand to pluck the notes on the high E, à la Eric Johnson.

LICK #6

A two-note per string fingering is used for the unusual pentatonic-like run in Lick #6. The notes in the pattern could be thought of as the B Hirajoshi scale (B–C#–D–F#–G) or the Gmaj7#11 arpeggio (G–B–D–F#–C#). This note combination can be used to emphasize the tension and color of the Phrygian mode. The line, as played here, consists of straightforward ascending-descending movement on the scale. However, notice the inclusion of the high A (♭3) note atop the second ascent of the pattern.

CHAPTER 5
PHRYGIAN DOMINANT MODE SOLOING ▶

PHRYGIAN DOMINANT OVERVIEW
- Phrygian Dominant is the fifth mode of the harmonic minor scale.
- The stepwise formula for Phrygian Dominant is: H–W+H–H–W–H–W–W.
- When compared to its parallel (from the same root) major scale, the degrees of Phrygian Dominant are numbered as follows: 1, ♭2, 3, 4, 5, ♭6, and ♭7.
- The "I" chord (or tonic) is typically a major triad, dominant 7th, or dominant 7♭9 chord.
- The three half-step intervals create extra tension in the Phrygian Dominant scale.

Compare the E Phrygian Dominant scale (fifth mode of A harmonic minor) with the standard E Phrygian scale (third mode of C major).

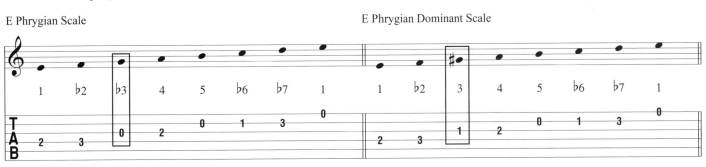

Typically, the major 3rd is responsible for a lift in the mood of the music. But, in the case of Phrygian Dominant, it also provides a new point of tension. This is due to the additional half-step interval that occurs between the third and fourth degrees. The augmented 2nd interval (one step) between the ♭2 and the major 3rd also creates a very stylized sound. When played as a static mode, the Phrygian Dominant scale can be used in a manner that suggests a Spanish or even Middle Eastern style.

PHRYGIAN DOMINANT SOLO
STUDY PREP
The example solo for this section uses the F♯ Phrygian Dominant scale (F♯–G–A♯–B–C♯–D–E), which is the fifth mode of B harmonic minor (B–C♯–D–E–F♯–G–A♯). The following patterns will help you prepare for learning the licks.

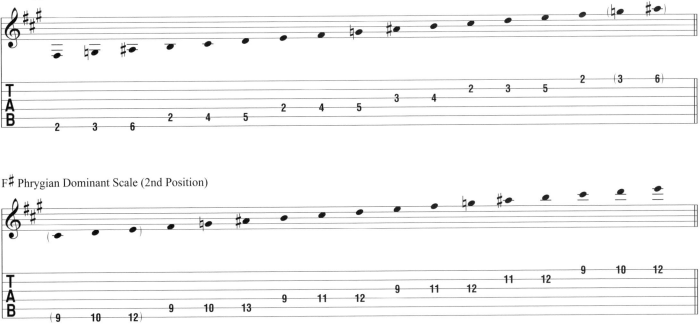

Any patterns you know for B harmonic minor can be used for the F♯ Phrygian Dominant scale. See the scale pattern section in the appendix of this book for more fingerings.

SOLO

Moderate Rock ♩ = 85

Lick #1

F#7♭9(no3rd)

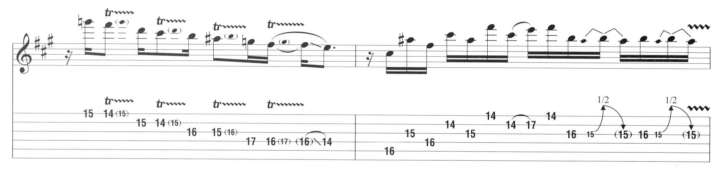

Lick #2

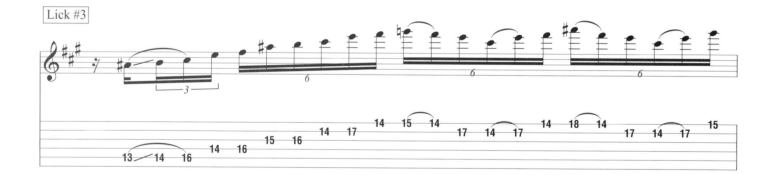

Lick #3

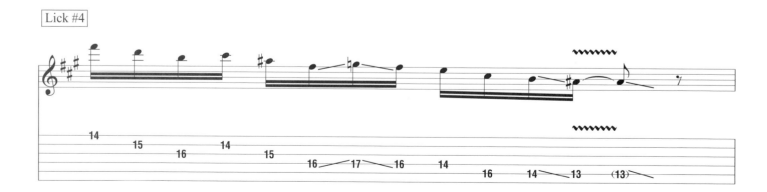

Lick #4

32

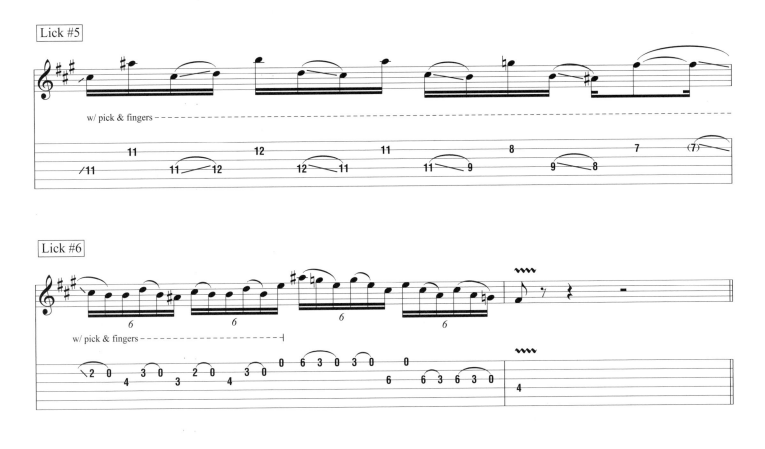

LICK #1

The scalar phrasing in Lick #1 makes use of a three-note per string pattern. This fingering is a result of omitting the ♭6 (D) of the scale. This six-note scale retains the primary color of Phrygian Dominant and yields a very useable fretboard shape.

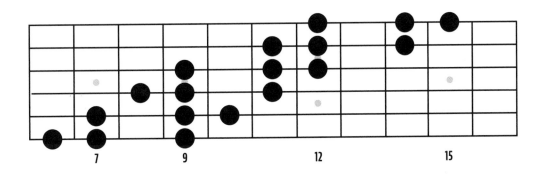

The first melodic sequence is repeated in the next octave, this time starting on the "and" of beat 4. This offsets the melody by a half-beat as it crosses into the second measure. The liberal use of slurs creates a "slinking" impression throughout the phrase.

LICK #2

Three half-step intervals occur within the Phrygian Dominant scale: 1–♭2, 3–4, and 5–♭6. Notice that the lower notes of each pair make up the tonic major triad. Each note of the F♯ major triad (F♯–A♯–C♯) is trilled with its upper neighbor in the first bar of Lick #2.

The same F♯ major triad position is used for the ascending intervallic sequence in the next measure. The quick half-step bends from the major 3rd (A♯) to the 4th (B) end the line.

LICK #3

The pentatonic oriented phrasing in Lick #3 is based on the F♯7(add4) arpeggio (F♯–A♯–B–C♯–E). This scale is also referred to as the Indian scale or the Dominant 11 Pentatonic scale. Notice the similarity of this pattern with F♯ minor pentatonic in the same position.

The ♭2 (G) is added for color in the repeating phrase over the last two bars. The high note is changed to the major 3rd (A♯) on the second repetition. The last note of the line (G) sets up the lick that follows.

LICK #4

The descending line in Lick #4 starts with two triad arpeggios: Bm and F♯ major. Breaking the scale up into its harmonic components like this is always a great way to employ the tonal variety within the mode. The end of the line is based on the F♯7(add4) arpeggio with the slide up to G added for color.

LICK #5

In Lick #5, shapes using intervals of a 6th are fingered along the fourth and second strings. The first major 6th interval of C♯ and A♯ implies the fifth and third degrees of the F♯ triad. Tension is produced when this shape is moved up a half-step to the D and G notes. After moving back down to the 11th-fret notes, the shapes adjust to the minor 6th interval shape on the B and G notes in beat 3, again producing tension. The line is briefly resolved into chord tones when this shape is shifted down to A♯ and F♯ in the last beat.

LICK #6

The last lick of the example solo starts with a series of open string pull-offs. The lick is based on the minor 3rd interval shape across the second and third strings. The B and D notes add tension to the phrase. The diminished 7th arpeggio (1, ♭3, ♭5, ♭♭7) occurs on the major 3rd of the Phrygian Dominant scale. This arpeggio is very popular for soloing over the scale. Its symmetrical interval structure (all minor 3rds) creates a distinct harmony, and it can be arranged into a variety of creative fingerings along the guitar's fretboard.

The second half of Lick #6 utilizes the A♯°7 (A♯–C♯–E–G) that is found within the F♯ Phrygian Dominant scale. The notes are arranged in a three-notes per string fingering, which allows for more legato articulation of the sequence.

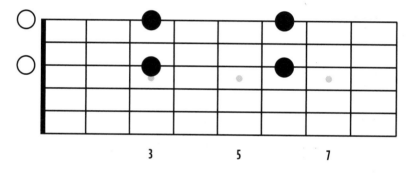

CHAPTER 6
LYDIAN MODE SOLOING ▶️

LYDIAN REVIEW

- Lydian is the fourth mode of the major scale.
- The stepwise formula for Lydian is W–W–W–H–W–W–H
- When compared to its parallel (from the same root) major scale, the degrees are numbered as follows: 1, 2, 3, ♯4, 5, 6, and 7.
- The "I" chord (or tonic) is typically a major triad, major 7th, or major 7♯11 chord.
- The ♯4 degree is the color tone of Lydian mode. Unlike the perfect 4th of the Ionian/major scale, the ♯4 does not tend to lead to the 3rd.

LYDIAN SOLO
STUDY PREP

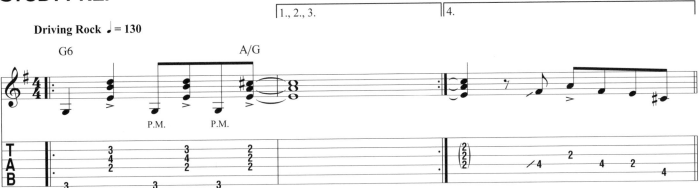

The example solo for this chapter was played over the rhythm figure above. This rhythm figure and the solo for the following section of this chapter uses the G Lydian mode (G–A–B–C♯–D–E–F♯). The repetitive low G in the bass, as well as the guitar riff shown here, keeps the tonality firmly grounded on the root. The G6 and A major triads are perceived as Lydian harmonies rather than an actual chord progression. The scale fragment in the fourth ending is from the F♯ minor pentatonic scale (F♯–A–B–C♯–E), which is present within G Lydian.

SCALE PATTERNS

In order to prepare for the examples from the solo, make sure to familiarize yourself with the following patterns for the G Lydian scale.

Since G Lydian is the fourth mode of the D major scale (D–E–F♯–G–A–B–C♯), the notes will be the same. Therefore, any patterns you know for the D major scale will be applicable to G Lydian.

G Lydian Scale (2nd Position)

G Lydian Scale (10th Position)

SOLO

Driving Rock ♩ = 130

Lick #1

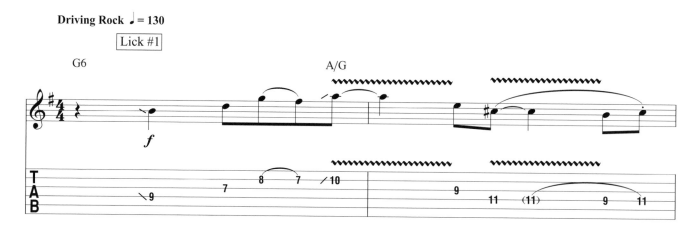

Lick #2

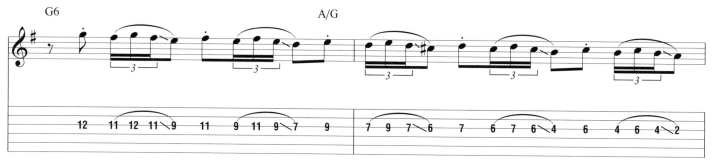

Lick #3

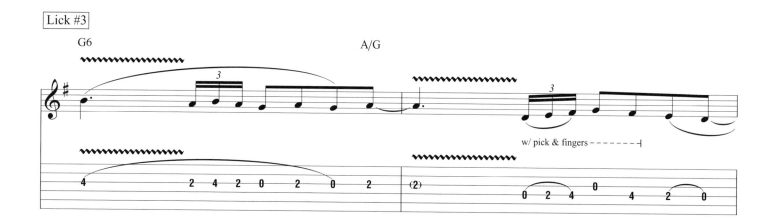

Lick #4

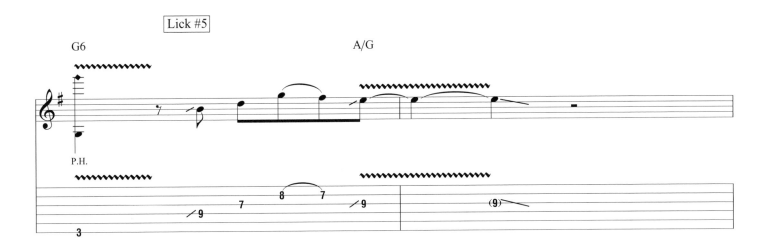

Lick #5

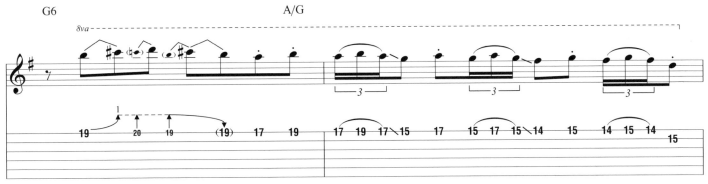

Lick #6

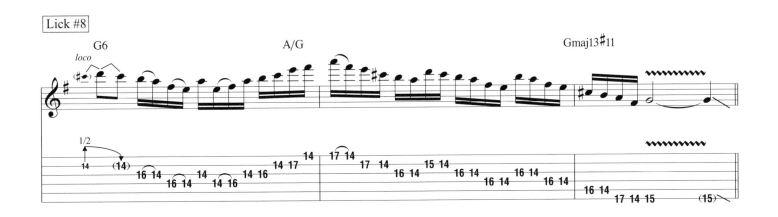

Lick #7

Lick #8

LICK #1

The first lick of the example solo makes use of chord tones on the G and A chords. A slide into the ninth-fret B initiates the 1st inversion G triad (B–D–G) shape. A pull-off to the major 7th (F♯) precedes the slide up to A, which coincides with the A/G chord in the riff. The descending A triad follows the same basic pattern as the G triad in measure 1.

LICK #2

The Django Reinhardt-inspired sequence in Lick #2 follows the G Lydian scale down the third string. Make sure you are comfortable visualizing the single-string scale pattern before working out the sequence. Since the root (G) falls on the open string and 12th fret, it is a simple matter of "seeing" the W–W–W–H–W–W–H (low to high) pattern.

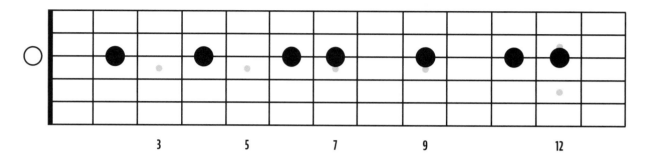

Starting on the "and" of beat 1, the 12th-fret root (G) is followed by a triplet hammer-on/pull-off from F♯ on beat 2. Without picking again, slide down to the next scale degree (E). The same series of articulations is then applied to the next group of notes in the scale, and so on. This figure is three eighth notes long in duration, so notice how it starts on alternating upbeats and downbeats as it proceeds.

LICK #3

The previous phrase lands on the B note that starts Lick #3. The first bar is a simple hammer-on/pull-off idea in the open position. Notice how it relates to the sequence in Lick #2. The inclusion of the second degree (A) foreshadows the A triad in the riff. The open-position scale fragment in the second bar leads to the next phrase.

LICK #4

Intervals of a 3rd are connected by open-string pull-offs in Lick #4. Make sure you can visualize the shapes of the 3rds of the G Lydian scale along these two strings. By adding a pull-off to each interval, the resulting three-note groups create a syncopated 16th-note rhythm.

The rapid-fire pull-offs in the second measure are reminiscent of a Randy Rhoads lick. Pick the first note of each string with a slight pinch harmonic for extra punch.

LICK #5

The seventh-position phrase in Lick #5 harkens back to the first lick of the solo. This time, the phrase ends with an E note held over the A/G chord.

LICK #6

The ascending line in the first measure of Lick #6 follows a simple fingering of the 12th and 14th frets across each string. A pair of six-note groups span the first three beats, creating rhythmic interest within the steady 16th-note subdivision. The segment that starts on beat 4 transitions into the regular scale shape with the slide into D at the top of measure 2. The scale continues on the first string with staccato eighth notes landing on the high-A target note.

LICK #7

The Lydian color tone (♯4) is prominent in the compound bend at the start of Lick #7. The scale sequence that follows in the second measure recaps the idea from Lick #2. This time, the phrase is descending the first string. Again, make sure you can easily visualize the basic pattern for the G Lydian scale along the single string.

LICK #8

The beginning of Lick #8 again emphasizes the ♯4 (C♯) with a quick bend up to D and back down. The scale sequence that follows is largely based on the F♯ minor pentatonic scale (F♯–A–B–C♯–E). Whenever playing in Lydian mode, the minor pentatonic that starts on the seventh degree can be used for great effect. Descending groups of six are used in the second measure. Notice the 15th-fret D that starts the second group on the "and" of beat 2. Beat 4 of the second measure begins the four-string descent that brings the solo to a close.

CHAPTER 7
MIXOLYDIAN MODE SOLOING

MIXOLYDIAN REVIEW

- Mixolydian is the fifth mode of the major scale.
- The stepwise formula for Mixolydian is: W–W–H–W–W–H–W.
- When compared to its parallel (from the same root) major scale, the degrees for the Mixolydian scale are: 1, 2, 3, 4, 5, 6, and ♭7.
- The "I" chord (or tonic) in Mixolydian is a dominant 7th chord (major-minor 7th chord).
- The Mixolydian has only one tension tone: the 4th (which leads to the 3rd).

Mixolydian is one of the three major modes indigenous to the major scale. Using the key of E, let's compare it to the parallel major.

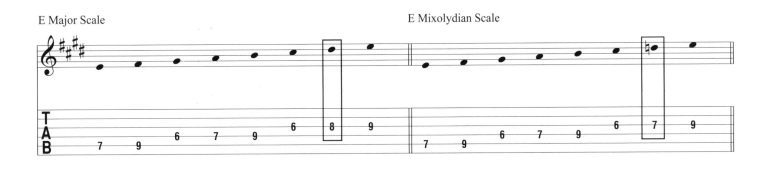

Play through the notes and pay attention to how lowering the seventh degree changes the mood of the scale. You might notice that the ♭7 tempers the enthusiasm of the Mixolydian scale when compared to the regular major scale.

TAKING ADVANTAGE OF PARALLEL AND DERIVATIVE THINKING FOR MIXOLYDIAN

You might recognize the preceding pattern as belonging to the key of A major, but try to realign your thinking to the key of E. When the phrasing or context suggests the root of E, your ear will naturally perceive the notes as they relate to E. Therefore, the key is heard as major with a flatted (minor) seventh degree (E Mixolydian). It can be very helpful to sing (or hum) along with the notes as you play through the scale pattern. Go back and forth between the E major and E Mixolydian scales, paying close attention to how the ♭7 degree changes the mood.

On the other hand, you can use the familiarity you might already have with major scale patterns to help facilitate your progress in finding the Mixolydian scale around the neck. Any A major scale position that you already know is also applicable to E Mixolydian. All the chords, arpeggios, pentatonic scales, etc., indigenous to A major can be used in E Mixolydian. Just realize that they will have a different effect when used in E Mixolydian.

By taking full advantage of both parallel and derivative perspectives, you will accelerate your learning process. The derivative method tells you that the E Mixolydian uses the same notes and patterns as the A major scale. The parallel method tells you that E Mixolydian sounds like an E major scale with a ♭7.

SOLOING OVER A ONE-CHORD MIXOLYDIAN VAMP
STUDY PREP

The example solo for this section is played over the following repetitive rhythm figure.

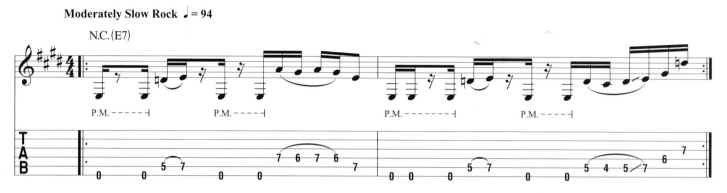

There is no substantial feeling of progression—just a static E7 key center that conveys the mood of Mixolydian. A static riff like this one provides an environment within which you can freely explore all the colors of the mode. The only tension in the mode exists with the fourth degree, which tends to lead down a half step to the major 3rd.

In preparation for learning the example solo, be sure to familiarize yourself with the following patterns for the E Mixolydian scale.

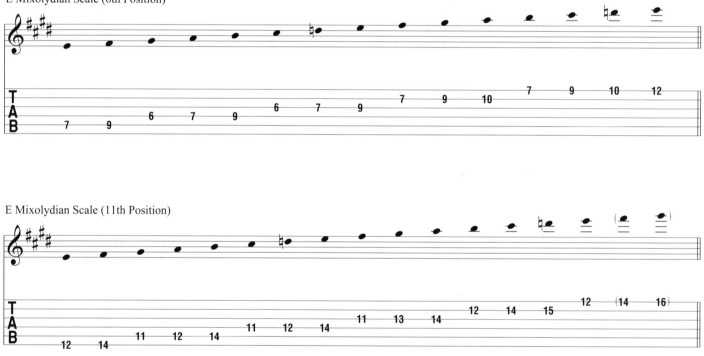

While the solo will make some use of other fingerings in E Mixolydian, these two positions provide good reference points to most of the content.

Be sure to watch the performance of the solo at the start of the video before proceeding with the lesson.

SOLO #1

Moderately Slow Rock ♩ = 94

Lick #1

N.C.(E7)

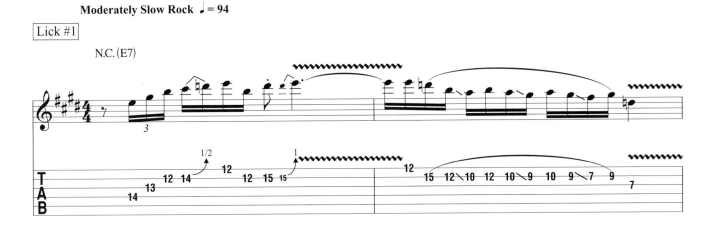

Lick #2

Lick #3

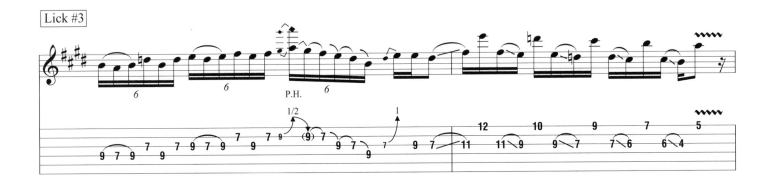

Lick #4

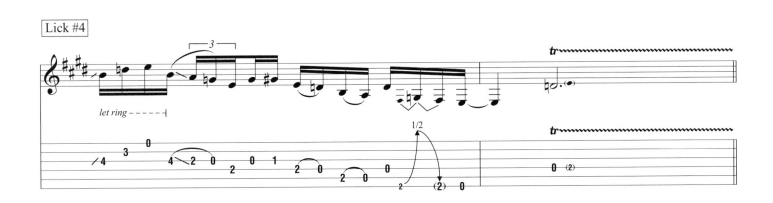

LICK #1

The first half of Lick #1 is based on a simple E7 arpeggio. A single downstroke is used to rake across the E triad (E–G#–B) to start the phrase. The major 6th (C#) is then bent into the b7 (D), giving the arpeggio a hint of extra color. The root and b7 are then mingled to accentuate the dominant chord sound.

The second half of Lick #1 is more scale-oriented. A fluid, legato effect is achieved by using slurred articulation along a single string. Take special care to play accurately and in time in order to convey the three-note groupings as they lay across the steady 16th-note subdivisions. The phrase ends by targeting the b7 for emphasis.

LICK #2

An angular line using the Indian pentatonic scale (1, 3, 4, 5, b7) starts the second lick of the solo. Notice that it's basically an E7 arpeggio (E–G#–B–D) with the fourth degree (A) added. The combination of slurs and picked notes bring out the interest in the rhythmic placement of interval skips. The line is then smoothed out by the purely stepwise movement (including the second degree, F#) at the end of the first measure.

The second measure of Lick #2 ramps up into a pair of sextuplet figures played across a simple two-note per string shape. Here, the naturally occurring pattern on the seventh and ninth frets can be thought of as melding the standard E dominant pentatonic (E–F#–G#–B–D) with the E Indian pentatonic (E–G#–A–B–D). A nice contrast to the previous phrase can be achieved by picking all the notes in this little sequence. The end of the lick is accentuated with a simple slide down to D, followed by the hammer-on and pull-off between the E and D.

LICK #3

The symmetrical, two-note per string shape is used for a classic Jimmy Page-style triplet sequence to start the next line. The bend to the fourth degree (A) provides a little tension on beat 3 before descending the pattern. Take care with the tricky articulation on beat 4.

The third line ends with a sequence of descending 7th intervals. Notice how the phrasing incorporates the slides rhythmically. Similar to the end of Lick #1, the groups of three should be played in a steady rhythm in order to hear the syncopated 16th-note subdivisions.

LICK #4

The last lick of the solo is an open-string blues phrase. Let the notes of the first beat ring together for maximum "twang." The bluesy sound of the G natural (open third string) adds a nice, stylistic flair to the lick. Use an aggressive touch throughout this line in order to put the exclamation point on the solo.

Blues licks can be very effective in the Mixolydian context. Just be aware that they will color the mood in a very stylistic way.

VIDEO BONUS LICK

The two-note per string sequence in the following lick is played with alternate picking for maximum impact. In beat 1, the initial four-note set is moved up one scale step for the second group. Only the top note of the group changes for each repetition through beat 2. This concept is carried into beat 3 with a move back to the seventh-position pattern. Moving down to the fifth position, the last group sets up an oscillation between the color tone (major 6th) and the minor 7th.

SOLOING OVER THE I–♭VII–IV PROGRESSION

The example solo for this section is played over the following rhythm figure.

D-A-D-G-B-E

All the notes and chords from the riff are indigenous to the D Mixolydian mode (D–E–F♯–G–A–B–C).

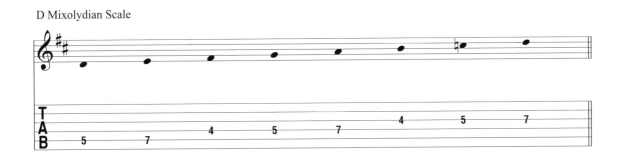

The I–♭VII–IV rhythm figure is a good example of the blending of tonal and modal concepts that frequently occurs in rock. The overall mood of the music is that of the Mixolydian mode. However, the movement from one chord to the next evokes the element of progression (moving away from and back to the tonic) that is associated with tonality.

While the Mixolydian mode is generally the correct scale for soloing over this entire rhythm figure, the notes of the scale will have a specific relationship to each chord. For this reason, it can be very effective to employ target notes from the underlying chord of the moment in your phrasing.

> The solo is located on the next page to allow for easier reading.

SOLO #2

Moderate Rock ♩ = 115

Lick #1

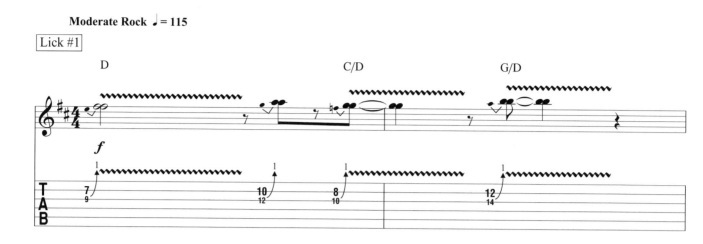

Lick #2

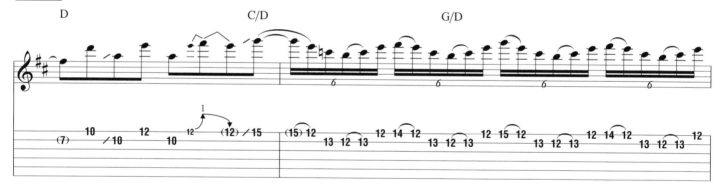

Lick #3

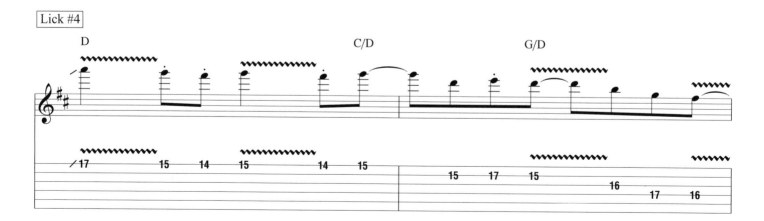

Lick #4

Lick #5

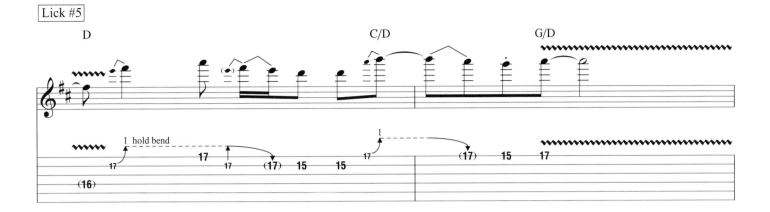

Lick #6

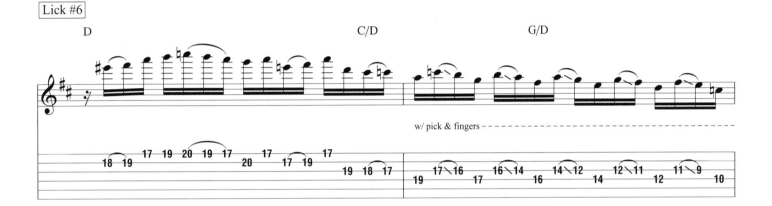

Lick #7

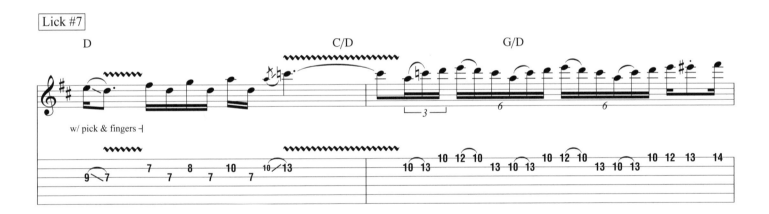

Lick #8

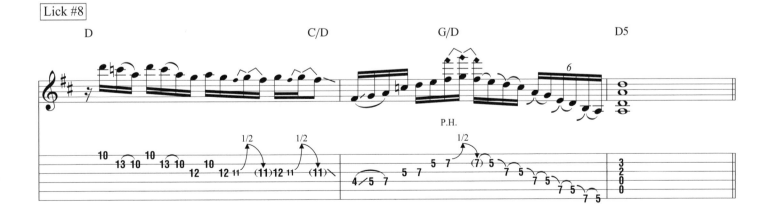

LICK #1

The solo starts with an ascending series of unison bends. Notice how the notes correspond with the notes in the chords at each point.

Over the D chord, unison bends are played on the 3rd (F♯) and the 5th (A) of the D chord. Anticipating the second measure is a bend to G. While this note is the fourth degree of the D Mixolydian scale, the importance here is the fact that it is the 5th of the C major triad (C–E–G). The last bend in the series is to B, the major 3rd of the G major triad (G–B–D).

LICK #2

The Indian pentatonic scale (1, 3, 4, 5, ♭7) is used for the ascending line in measure 1 of the second lick. The notes outline a D7 chord with the 4th added for tension and color. This ascending run targets the C major chord tone, G, before descending to the B and G notes on the G chord (the 3rd and root, respectively). The F♯ at the end of the measure anticipates the return to the D chord at the start of the next line.

LICK #3

A pivot from the 5th (A) starts Lick #3. The bend targets the 3rd, F♯. The 16th-note triplet figure that follows is based on a Cmaj7 arpeggio (C–E–G–B). Notice that the high note alternates between G and F♯, playing off the tension and color of the 6th and ♭7 in the Mixolydian mode. When the chord changes to G underneath, the lick remains static, thereby producing more tension.

LICK #4

The tension from the previous lick is briefly resolved with a slide to the 5th (A) of the D chord at the start of Lick #4. The interplay between the F♯ and G notes then resumes.

The slide up to the G at the end of the first bar is timely, as it is the target note for the C chord. A variation of this melodic idea is then connected to the descending G triad (D–G–B) to end the phrase. The upcoming D chord is again anticipated with the F♯ at the end of this line.

LICK #5

The bending lick in first bar of Lick #5 is centered around the notes of the D triad (D–F♯–A). However, the phrasing for the second half of the lick does not target triad tones on the C and G chords. Instead, the note choices add color.

The focal point (high note) of the phrase is the bend to B over the C chord (the major 7th of the chord). The A note at the end of the line is the 9th of the G chord, but it is heard more as the fifth degree of D Mixolydian. This departure from chord-tone targets frees up the phrasing a bit, avoiding predictability.

LICK #6

The first measure of Lick #6 employs a couple of bluesy/jazzy ideas. The ♯9 (E♯) at the beginning of the phrase could also be thought of as the minor 3rd (F) of D. Blending the minor and major 3rds over a major chord creates a very bluesy sound. This unaccented passing tone is immediately hammered into the major 3rd (F♯) at the start of the line.

At the end of the first bar, you'll notice the use of the major 7th (C♯) as a passing tone that connects the root (D) to the ♭7 (C). While its use here is not strictly according to historical jazz stylings, it alludes to the Bebop Mixolydian scale (1, 2, 3, 4, 5, 6, ♭7, ♮7, R). The major 7th creates a nice tension that precedes the ♭7 when descending from the root.

The descending line in the second bar is based on a sequence of 3rds that harmonizes the scale along the third and fourth strings. Make sure to keep the slides in steady rhythm in order to nail the 16th-note timing.

LICK #7

Another pivot idea, similar to the one in Lick #3, starts the next line. The pivot from the root (D) is juxtaposed with a short, scalar ascent to the ♭7 (C). The C is held as it is transformed by the harmonic progression, becoming the root of the C chord underneath.

The repetitive figure in the second bar is derived from the D dominant pentatonic scale (D–E–F♯–A–C). This static lick builds tension before ending with the bluesy chromaticism at the end of the line.

LICK #8

The last line of the solo starts with a phrase from the D Indian or Dominant 11th Pentatonic scale (D–F#–G–A–C). Take care with the tricky bending at the end of measure 1.

The 6th (B) of D Mixolydian is skipped in the scalar ascent in measure 2. The focal-point bend to G corresponds with the G chord before quickly descending the symmetrical, two-note per string pattern to end the solo. Notice that all notes are slurred (no picking) for the descent.

CHAPTER 8
AEOLIAN MODE SOLOING ▶️

AEOLIAN REVIEW

- Aeolian is the sixth mode of the major scale. It is the same as **relative minor**. It is also called the **natural minor** or **pure minor**.
- The stepwise formula for the Aeolian scale is: W–H–W–W–H–W–W.
- When compared to its parallel major scale (from the same root), the degrees are: 1, 2, ♭3, 4, 5, ♭6, and ♭7.
- The "I" chord (or tonic) is a minor triad or minor 7th chord.
- The tension tone in Aeolian is the ♭6 degree, which resolves down a half step to the 5th.

MINOR KEY TONALITY VS. AEOLIAN MODE

Tonal music, like that of typical major and minor keys, makes use of tension and release to create motion in melodies and chord progressions. Purely modal music is more static in nature. By remaining anchored to the root note, the colors inherent to the mode are exploited without the need to create motion through tension and release. In the case of Aeolian, the ♭6 would not necessarily be used to generate energy to move to the fifth degree, either in the melody or chord harmony. As with all notes in the mode, it could be used somewhat freely for its unique color.

In modern application, however, these lines between modal and tonal music are frequently blurred. By combining tonal concepts (tension/release and chord progression) with modal principles (free use of color tones and chord extensions), the possibilities are greatly increased in modern music. Our study of the Aeolian mode in this book will reflect this blended approach.

A minor is the relative minor/Aeolian mode of C major.

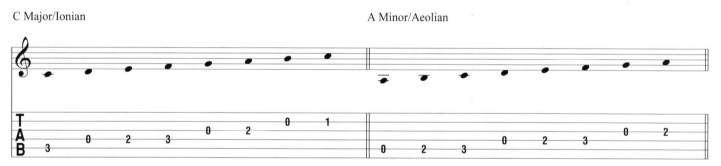

C Major/Ionian   A Minor/Aeolian

Any patterns that you know for the minor scale will be the same for the Aeolian mode, since they are the same notes.

AEOLIAN SOLO OVER CHORDS FROM NATURAL MINOR
STUDY PREP

The examples for the rest of this chapter use the F♯ Aeolian mode (F♯–G♯–A–B–C♯–D–E). The example solo for this chapter was played over the following rhythm figures.

Rhythm Figure 1

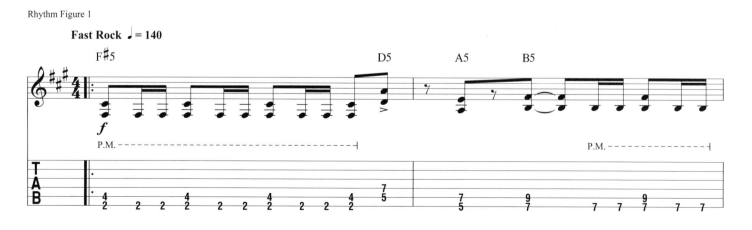

Rhythm Figure 2

All the notes in the chords and riffs are indigenous to the F# Aeolian mode.

SCALE PATTERNS

In preparation for learning the licks from the example solo for this chapter, make sure you are familiar with the following patterns of the F# Aeolian scale.

F# Aeolian/Natural Minor Scale (2nd Position)

F# Aeolian/Natural Minor Scale (9th Position)

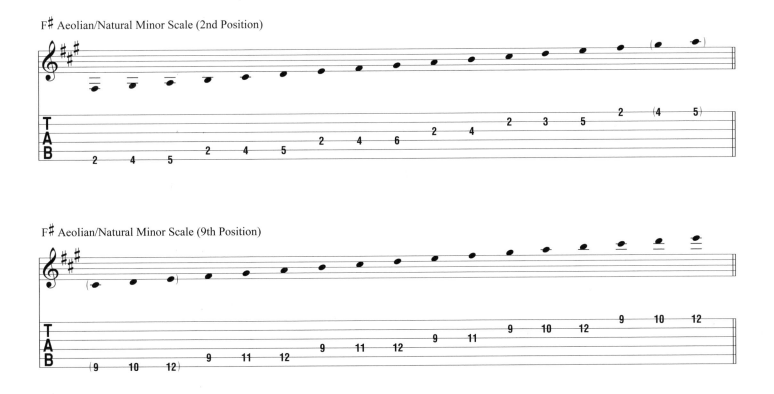

SOLO

Fast Rock ♩ = 140

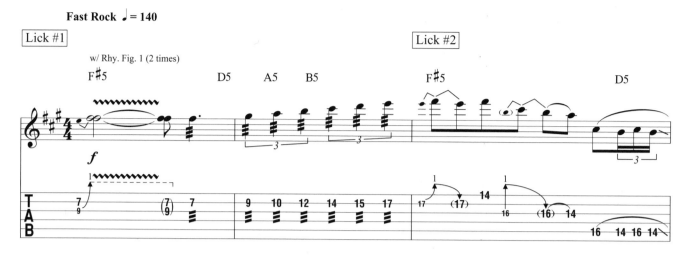

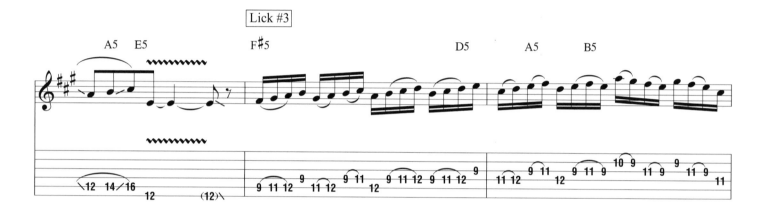

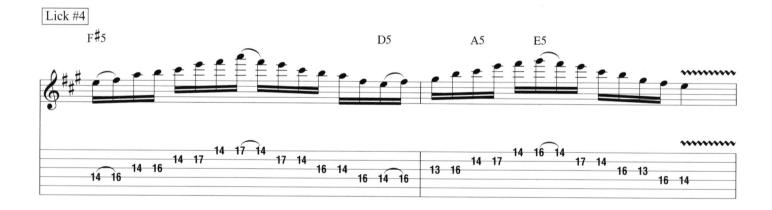

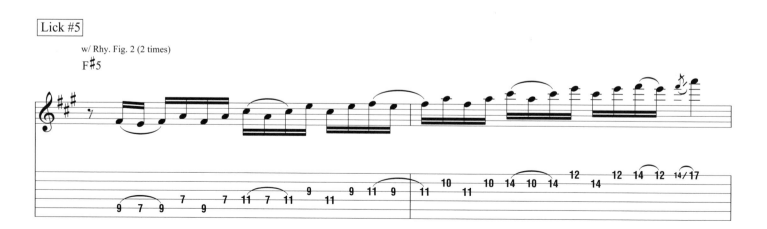

Lick #6

Lick #7

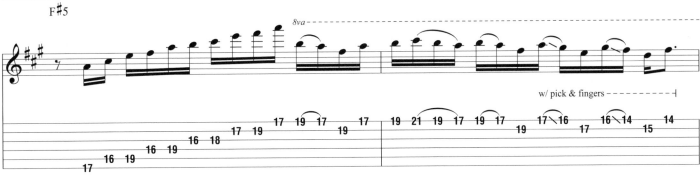

Lick #8

Lick #9

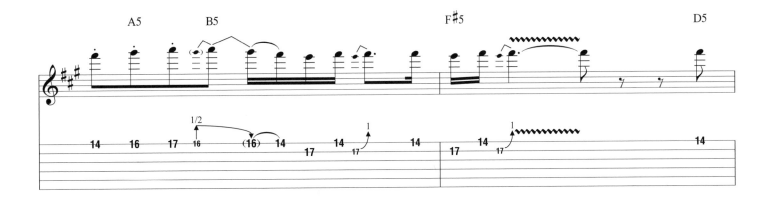

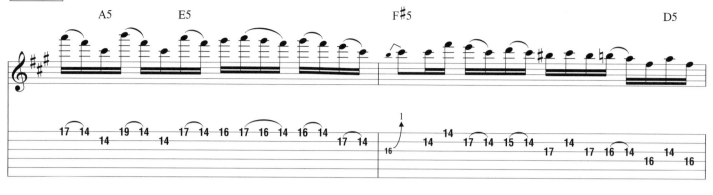

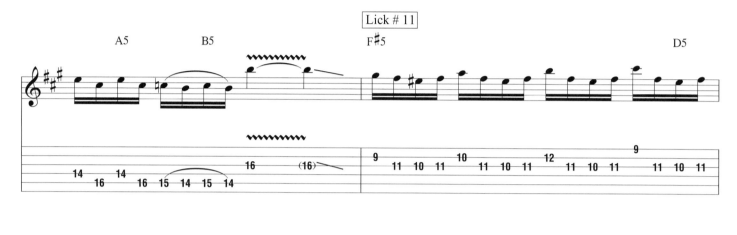

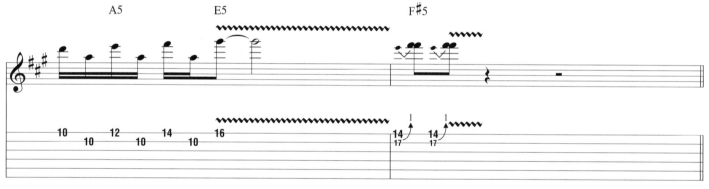

LICK #1

The solo begins with a unison bend on the root (F♯). The ninth-fret, third-string E is bent up a whole step to match the pitch of the second-string F♯. The tremolo picking that starts on the F♯ at the end of measure 1 is continued throughout the ascending scale in measure 2. The notes simply climb the F♯ Aeolian scale in a quarter-note triplet rhythm. The tremolo picking is in free time—just pick as fast as you want for each pitch.

LICK #2

The Michael Schenker-influenced phrase in Lick #2 is based in the F♯ minor pentatonic scale (F♯–A–B–C♯–E). By first bending to the root and then the 5th (C♯), the beginning of the phrase relates strongly to the F♯5 chord underneath. The fourth string is skipped, providing intervallic interest as the lick descends to the C♯ on beat 4.

The hammer-ons and pull-offs along the fifth string make the end of the pentatonic line fluid. The phrase ends with the root of the underlying E5 chord.

LICK #3

The ninth-position pattern for the F♯ Aeolian scale is used for the sequencing line in Lick #3. The line starts with a basic sequencing in groups of four. Each downbeat starts a new segment starting on successive degrees of the scale. This sequence carries over into the second measure with a slight change at the end of beat 2. The sequences change to descending fours on beats 3 and 4.

While this lick could just as well be played with all picking, I chose to incorporate a number of slurs. Notice how the mix of hammer-ons, pull-offs, and picked notes creates interest in the articulation.

LICK #4
The Aeolian mode contains three different minor pentatonic scales. They are found starting from the root, fourth degree, and fifth degree. Within the F# Aeolian mode, we will find F# minor pentatonic (F#–A–B–C#–E), B minor pentatonic (B–D–E–F#–A) and C# minor pentatonic (C#–E–F#–G#–B).

Lick #4 starts with an ascending and descending run along the 14th-position F# minor pentatonic scale (starting on the fourth string, E), followed by a similar run up and down the C# pentatonic scale in the same position. The C# minor pentatonic could be thought of as E major pentatonic since it relates to the E5 chord of the riff.

LICK #5
The F#m7 arpeggio in Lick #5 is fingered in a two-note per string pattern. This fingering allows for the Jimmy Page-style sequence to be applied in the same manner as the common pentatonic run. It can be very helpful to work out the basic pattern before applying the sequence.

The sequence itself is a series of three-note groupings. However, the timing is in a steady 16th-note subdivision. This creates a nice syncopation as the line unfolds. Be sure to practice with a metronome in order to nail the timing.

LICK #6
The E5 chord of the riff is highlighted by the Paul Gilbert-style E major arpeggio (E–G#–B) that sequences in Lick #6. Again, it can be helpful to study the basic fingering pattern of the arpeggio before working on the specific sequencing. Here, the 12th-position E major arpeggio is arranged in a string-skipping pattern. Notice that, by placing the B note on the 16th fret of the third string (instead of the 12th fret of the second string), the arpeggio can be played with a more legato approach. Throughout the two-measure phrase, anytime there are two successive notes on a string, the second is played with a slur.

The triplet sequencing begins in the first measure with a pair of descending three-note groups, starting on the high G#, then starting on E. Beats 3 and 4 consist of a simple ascent/descent of the one-octave arpeggio. That six-note phrase is played again at the start of bar 2, but the timing is ramped up to 16th notes. The line ends with the two descending groups of three (still played in 16th-note timing) that land on the root of the E chord at beat 4.

LICK #7
A run up the 16th-position F# minor scale starts Lick #7. Notice that the 19th-fret B note is skipped on the low E string of the pattern. The resulting F#m7 chord tones (A–C#–E–F#) make a strong reference to the tonic chord in the riff at the beginning of the line.

The continuation of pentatonic phrasing in measure 2 eventually gives way to a descending Aeolian sequence, shifting down the first and second strings. Notice how the colors introduced by the 2nd (G#) and b6 (D) in the last two beats bring out the moodiness of the line.

LICK #8
With the E5 chord in the riff, the solo again centers around the E major arpeggio (E–G#–B) at the start of Lick #8. The descending line in the first measure can be seen as three segments of the E triad. Starting with the 16th-position fingering, the arpeggio descends into two successive slides along the third string in beat 2. Notice the A on the 14th fret, as it adds color to the arpeggio while connecting the pattern. The 13th-position E triad fingering is then encountered, starting with the third string, G#. Use the second finger to barre across the 14th-fret E and B notes. On the fifth string, arrive at the next three-note shift, again including the A note in order to connect. This part of the lick ends with a climb from the 12th fret, low E string, through the shell of an E7 chord.

In the second measure of the Lick #8, the E7 sound transitions into more of the available F# Aeolian colors with a descending D major 7th arpeggio (D–F#–A–C#) on beat 2. This phrase drops into a scale fragment on the way down to the root (F#) at the top of the next measure.

LICK #9

The F#m(add9) arpeggio (F#–G#–A–C#) is the main concept featured in Lick #9. The fingering is easily visualized as being arranged in pairs of strings. The root (F#), 2nd (G#) and ♭3rd (A) will be on the lowest string of each pair, the 5th (C#) on the higher string. This arrangement starts on the fifth string, ninth fret, on beat 1 and continues across the first two beats. The pattern then starts over on the third beat with the third-string, 11th-fret F# on beat 3. The use of legato phrasing in the first octave and staccato phrasing in the next provides contrast to the articulation.

The staccato phrasing continues in the next measure with the ascent to the high A on the first string. That minor 3rd is the focal point of the line, even though the chord changes to B5 underneath. At this point, the phrasing targets the tonic chord (F#m) with less regard to the changing chords in the riff. The bending phrase at the end of the lick is repeated in a syncopated manner. This results in "playing over the bar line," which takes us into the first bar of the next repetition of the riff.

LICK #10

The second and lowered sixth degrees of the Aeolian mode are selectively incorporated into minor pentatonic and blues scale phrases in Lick #10. In the first bar, ascending high notes pivot off the barred 14th-fret F# and C# in order to generate energy before moving into linear phrasing in beats 3 and 4. The G# adds color to the otherwise minor pentatonic passage.

The next two bars feature a Randy Rhoads-inspired phrase. A classic Chuck Berry-style bend initiates the line. As the phrasing moves down the 14th-position F# blues scale (F#–A–B–C♮–C#–E), the ♭6th (D) is added on the second string, bringing out the dark mood of Aeolian.

LICK #11

The pivot lick ideas in Lick #11 are in the style of Yngwie Malmsteen. The major 7th (E#) is used in the first bar. This alludes to the F# harmonic minor scale (F#–G#–A–B–C#–D–E#). Notice how this creates a lot of energy around the root (F#) in the pivot of the lick. Against this three-note pivot is a simple ascending scale passage starting on G#.

The second measure of Lick #11 continues the scalar ascent with a single-note pivot from the second-string, tenth-fret A. Notice that notes have changed back to F# Aeolian (from harmonic minor) as the line goes over the A5 and E5 chords, both of which contain E natural. The solo ends with unison bends on the accented F#.

FURTHER EXPLORATION OF THE AEOLIAN MODE

The examples shown here reflect a situation in which modal concepts are blended with tonal concepts, like chord progression and tension/release. Be sure to practice using these Aeolian scale ideas over a static root note (like a droning bass note) or F#m chord for a purer modal experience.

CHAPTER 9
LOCRIAN MODE SOLOING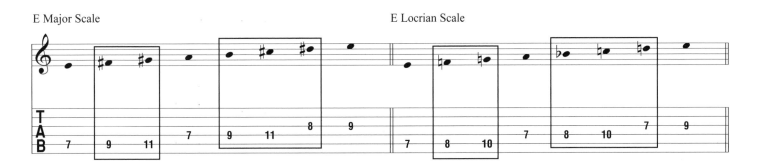

LOCRIAN REVIEW

- Locrian is the seventh mode of the major scale.
- The stepwise formula for Locrian is: H–W–W–H–W–W–W.
- When compared to its parallel major scale, the degrees for the Locrian scale are: 1, ♭2, ♭3, 4, ♭5, ♭6, and ♭7.
- The "I" chord (or tonic) is a diminished triad or minor 7♭5 chord. In traditional theory, this is not a legitimate tonic chord, as it is not resolved.
- The ♭2 tends to lead down to the root. The ♭6 degree can be tricky to handle, being that it is a tension tone with no perfect 5th in the scale to lead to.

Compare E Locrian to its parallel major scale and notice how unstable it sounds.

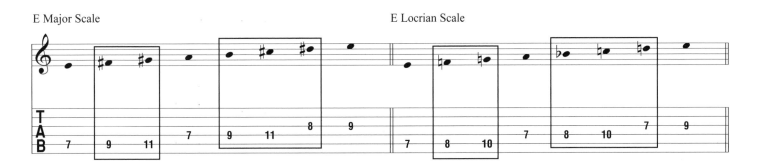

Locrian is unique among the modes of the major scale in that it has an unresolved harmony for its "tonic" chord (due to the ♭5). Therefore, the application of Locrian for the key center defies the standards of tonicization (resolution). The more common use for the Locrian scale is in applying it to the minor 7♭5 (also called "half-diminished") chord in a tonal chord progression.

In this context, the use of the Locrian scale is not truly modal in nature. More accurately, it is being used as a resource for notes that harmonize "correctly" with the chord underneath. Once the progression moves to the next chord (V7), the scale resource changes to fit. In this way, the appropriate mode for each chord is used to shape the melodic line over a tonal chord progression. Simply put: the scales fit the chords.

While the use of modes for soloing over tonal chord progressions is an important skill, in this lesson, we will explore the application of Locrian mode for its tension over a one-chord vamp or riff.

TAKING ADVANTAGE OF PARALLEL AND DERIVATIVE THINKING FOR LOCRIAN

When you played the E Locrian scale earlier, you probably noticed that it has the same notes as F major. And any fretboard pattern for E Locrian looks the same as F major. Following this derivative method, you could simply go up a half-step from any root and play a major scale in order to produce the Locrian mode. Just remember that the seventh degree of that major scale will be the root of your Locrian mode (E is the seventh degree of F major).

As with any major scale mode, the derivative method is a quick way to identify patterns on the fretboard. But in order to truly understand the sound, we'll need to spend time relating the notes to the modal root. By comparing the Locrian scale degrees with those of the parallel major scale, we get the formula of 1, b2, b3, 4, b5, b6, and b7.

With all the tension and instability, you might find the process of anchoring your ear on the Locrian root a bit challenging. Since the b5 is the only difference in degree formulas between the Phrygian and Locrian modes, it can be helpful to think of the Locrian as a slightly altered Phrygian scale. Compare the E Locrian with the E Phrygian scale.

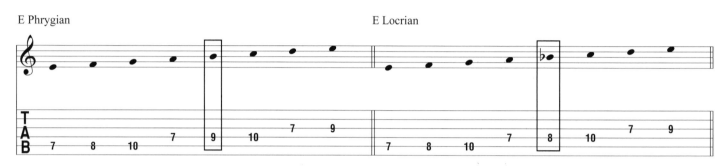

Play the notes of each scale, then sing (or hum) them. The relevance of relating the Locrian scale to its parallel Phrygian will become even more apparent as we explore how it is often used in a rock/metal context.

LOCRIAN SOLO
STUDY PREP
The example solo for this section will be played over the following rhythm figure.

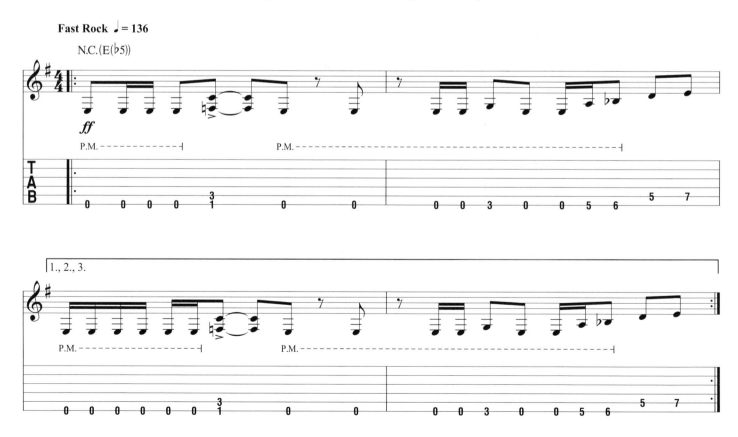

All the notes in this riff are indigenous to E Locrian, with the exception of the very last chord, E5 (which contains a B natural). In spite of this, the strong impression of a key center seems to suggest E Phrygian. Notice that the ♭6 (C) of the scale is only used when it is part of the F5 chord. By only employing this note sparingly, some of the instability inherent in Locrian mode is alleviated.

SCALE PATTERNS

In preparation for learning the example solo, familiarize yourself with the following patterns for E Locrian.

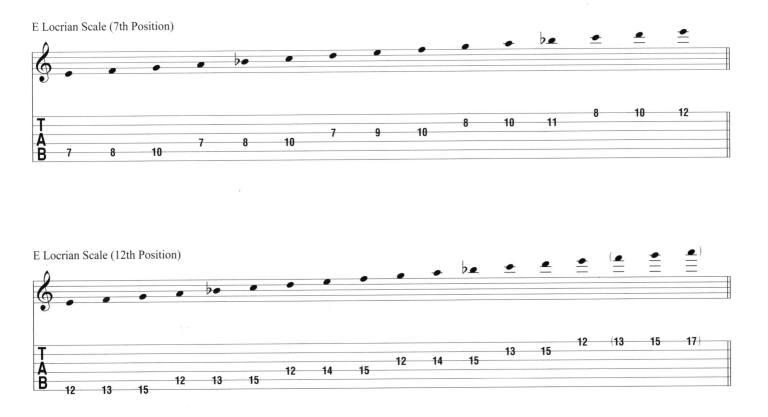

The solo will venture outside these two positions, but they will make good reference points as you connect the ideas. Be sure to watch the video performance of the solo before proceeding with the next part of the lesson.

The solo is located on the next page to allow for easier reading.

SOLO

Fast Rock ♩ = 136

Lick #1

N.C. E(♭5)

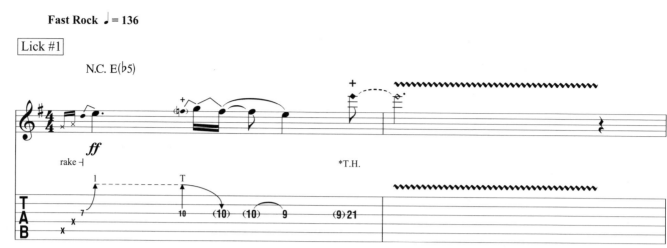

*Lightly touch string at 21st fret to sound harmonic.

Lick #2

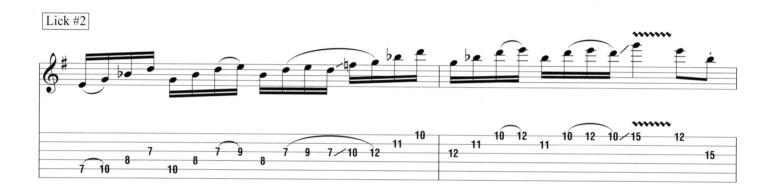

Lick #3

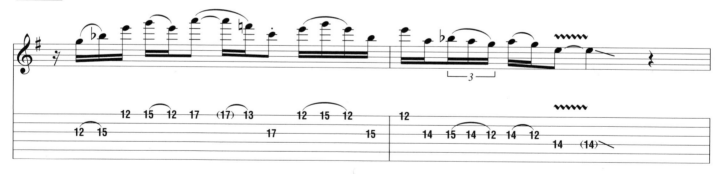

Lick #4

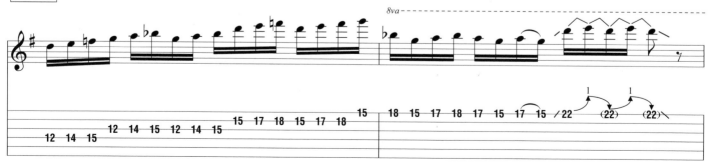

Lick #5

Lick #6

Lick #7

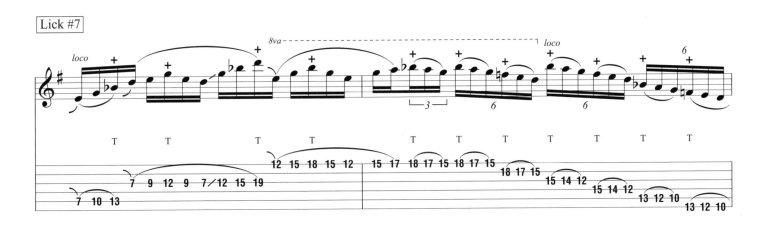

Lick #8

LICK #1

The solo starts with an interplay of the root (E) and ♭2 (F). Immediately after tapping the tenth fret, the left hand releases the bend and shifts to fret the ninth fret in preparation for the right-hand pull-off. The harmonic of the fretted E is then tapped with the right hand at the 21st fret.

LICK #2

The sequence in the next two bars is based on the Em7♭5 arpeggio. The rhythmic placement of the slurs adds interest to the articulation, changing up the otherwise predictable nature of the straight "fours."

Notice the use of the F (♭2) on beat 4 of the first measure. Not only does this note make the shift more comfortable, it also adds a little hint of extra color to the arpeggio.

LICK #3

The arpeggiation is continued in the beginning of the third lick. String skipping helps to facilitate clear rhythmic execution on the E diminished triad (E–G–B♭) in the first measure.

This string-skipping idea is then sequenced up to an F major triad (F–A–C) and back to E diminished. The addition of the fourth degree (A) in the short, scalar ending evokes a bit of the blues scale.

LICK #4

As mentioned earlier, the ♭6 of the Locrian scale can be a tricky to apply in this context. For this reason, it could be thought of as an avoid note. The linear sequence in the next example is based on a repeating whole-step/half-step pattern that travels across the top four strings.

The first three beats are divided into two groups of six 16th notes, giving a little syncopation to the steady subdivision. A neoclassical-inspired phrase caps off the ascent. The bent note at the end should be conceived as a slow, wide vibrato.

LICK #5

The energy is sustained in the fifth line of the solo with a two-note per string picking lick inspired by Randy Rhoads. In measure 1, the first note of each repeating group alternates between the 4th (A) and ♭5 (B♭).

The steady 16th notes get syncopated accents in measure 2 when the sequence is varied by doubling up on the first string on beat 1 and again on the "and" of beat 3. It can be challenging to pick this lick cleanly. Some guitarists find it easier to start picking with a downstroke, and some find it easier to start with an upstroke. Be sure to try both ways in order find out what works best for you.

LICK #6

A simple tremolo picking idea along the first string keeps the energy up while opening up the melodic space of the solo in the phrase. The line is comprised of a simple Em7♭5 arpeggio (E–B♭–D) sequence. Use the same finger throughout in order to get the most audible slides into each note.

LICK #7

Two-handed tapping is exclusively employed in Lick #7. Before attempting to play the first half of the lick, spend a little time getting familiar with the locations and patterns of the notes. Starting with an Em7♭5 arpeggio arranged into a pair of connected string skipping shapes, the two halves of this measure are easily separated for practice.

Take care to keep the strings quiet, as you will need to "hammer-on from nowhere" with the left hand to initiate the notes of each string. This technique is somewhat contrary to the classic approach to starting each new string with the tapping hand. As always, metronome practice is essential for establishing good timing and accuracy.

The descending scale run in the second measure is based on the symmetrical pattern we encountered in Lick #4, again avoiding the ♭6 (C). Notice how tapping is utilized for maximum fluidity and speed in this permutation. Resolution of the lick occurs with the root (E) on the downbeat of Lick #8.

LICK #8

The sample solo closes with a spacious yet aggressive phrase that links up with the accompaniment's ending riff. The descending scalar phrase has a rock attitude, and it could be thought of as having been derived from the blues scale (without the perfect 5th).

APPENDIX

MAJOR SCALE PATTERNS

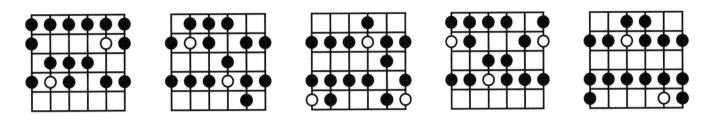

HARMONIC MINOR SCALE PATTERNS

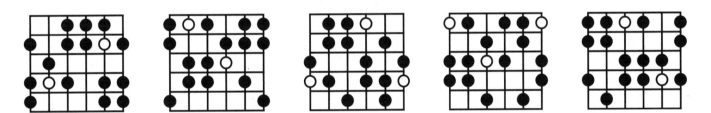

MELODIC MINOR SCALE PATTERNS

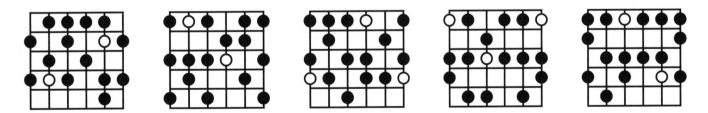

COMMON SCALE/MODE FORMULAS

MODES OF THE MAJOR SCALE:
1. Ionian/Major Scale: 1, 2, 3, 4, 5, 6, 7
2. Dorian Scale: 1, 2, ♭3, 4, 5, 6, ♭7
3. Phrygian Scale: 1, ♭2, ♭3, 4, 5, ♭6, ♭7
4. Lydian Scale: 1, 2, 3, ♯4, 5, 6, 7
5. Mixolydian Scale: 1, 2, 3, 4, 5, 6, ♭7
6. Aeolian Scale: 1, 2, ♭3, 4, 5, ♭6, ♭7
7. Locrian Scale: 1, ♭2, ♭3, 4, ♭5, ♭6, ♭7

MODES OF THE HARMONIC MINOR SCALE:
1. Harmonic Minor Scale: 1, 2, ♭3, 4, 5, ♭6, 7
2. Locrian Natural 6 Scale: 1, ♭2, ♭3, 4, ♭5, 6, ♭7
3. Ionian Augmented Scale: 1, 2, 3, 4, ♯5, 6, 7
4. Dorian ♯4 Scale: 1, 2, ♭3, ♯4, 5, 6, ♭7
5. Phrygian Dominant Scale: 1, ♭2, 3, 4, 5, ♭6, ♭7
6. Lydian ♯2 Scale: 1, ♯2, 3, ♯4, 5, 6, 7
7. Super Locrian ♭♭7 Scale: 1, ♭2, ♭3, ♭4, ♭5, ♭6, ♭♭7

MODES OF THE MELODIC MINOR SCALE:
1. Melodic Minor Scale (Ascending): 1, 2, ♭3, 4, 5, 6, 7
2. Dorian ♭2 Scale: 1, ♭2, ♭3, 4, 5, 6, ♭7
3. Lydian Augmented Scale: 1, 2, 3, ♯4, ♯5, 6, 7
4. Lydian Dominant Scale: 1, 2, 3, ♯4, 5, 6, ♭7
5. Mixolydian ♭6 Scale: 1, 2, 3, 4, 5, ♭6, ♭7
6. Locrian Natural 2 Scale: 1, 2, ♭3, 4, ♭5, ♭6, ♭7
7. Super Locrian/Altered Dominant Scale: 1, ♭2, ♭3, ♭4, ♭5, ♭6, ♭7

COMMON PENTATONIC SCALES:
- Minor Pentatonic Scale: 1, ♭3, 4, 5, ♭7
- Major Pentatonic Scale: 1, 2, 3, 5, 6
- Dominant Pentatonic Scale: 1, 2, 3, 5, ♭7
- Indian/Dominant 11th Pentatonic Scale: 1, 3, 4, 5, ♭7
- Hirajoshi Scale: 1, 2, ♭3, 5, ♭6

OTHER SCALES:
- Blues Scale: 1, ♭3, ♮4, ♯4, 5, ♭7
- Major Blues Scale: 1, ♮2, ♯2, 3, 5, 6
- Diminished Scale: 1, 2, ♭3, 4, ♭5, ♭6, ♮6, 7
- Half-Whole Diminished Scale: 1, ♭2, ♭3, ♮3, ♯4, 5, 6, ♭7
- Hungarian Minor Scale: 1, 2, ♭3, ♯4, 5, ♭6, 7
- Hungarian Gypsy Scale: 1, ♭2, 3, 4, 5, ♭6, 7
- Harmonic Major Scale: 1, 2, 3, 4, 5, ♭6, 7
- Bebop Major Scale: 1, 2, 3, 4, 5, ♯5, 6, 7
- Bebop Dorian Scale: 1, 2, ♭3, ♮3, 4, 5, 6, ♭7
- Bebop Mixolydian/Dominant Scale: 1, 2, 3, 4, 5, 6, ♭7, ♮7

GUITAR NOTATION LEGEND

Guitar music can be notated three different ways: on a *musical staff*, in *tablature*, and in *rhythm slashes*.

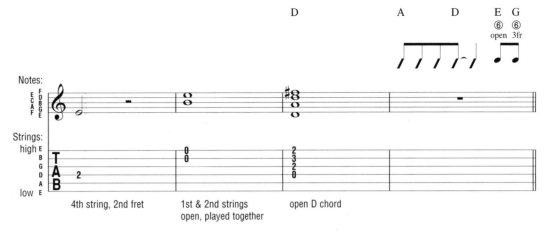

RHYTHM SLASHES are written above the staff. Strum chords in the rhythm indicated. Use the chord diagrams found at the top of the first page of the transcription for the appropriate chord voicings. Round noteheads indicate single notes.

THE MUSICAL STAFF shows pitches and rhythms and is divided by bar lines into measures. Pitches are named after the first seven letters of the alphabet.

TABLATURE graphically represents the guitar fingerboard. Each horizontal line represents a string, and each number represents a fret.

4th string, 2nd fret   1st & 2nd strings open, played together   open D chord

Definitions for Special Guitar Notation

HALF-STEP BEND: Strike the note and bend up 1/2 step.

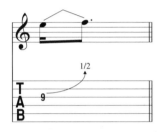

WHOLE-STEP BEND: Strike the note and bend up one step.

GRACE NOTE BEND: Strike the note and immediately bend up as indicated.

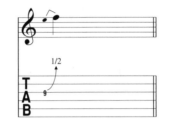

SLIGHT (MICROTONE) BEND: Strike the note and bend up 1/4 step.

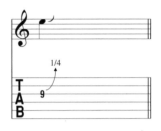

BEND AND RELEASE: Strike the note and bend up as indicated, then release back to the original note. Only the first note is struck.

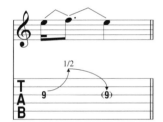

PRE-BEND: Bend the note as indicated, then strike it.

PRE-BEND AND RELEASE: Bend the note as indicated. Strike it and release the bend back to the original note.

UNISON BEND: Strike the two notes simultaneously and bend the lower note up to the pitch of the higher.

VIBRATO: The string is vibrated by rapidly bending and releasing the note with the fretting hand.

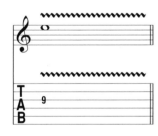

WIDE VIBRATO: The pitch is varied to a greater degree by vibrating with the fretting hand.

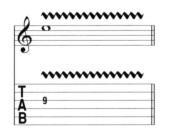

HAMMER-ON: Strike the first (lower) note with one finger, then sound the higher note (on the same string) with another finger by fretting it without picking.

PULL-OFF: Place both fingers on the notes to be sounded. Strike the first note and without picking, pull the finger off to sound the second (lower) note.

LEGATO SLIDE: Strike the first note and then slide the same fret-hand finger up or down to the second note. The second note is not struck.

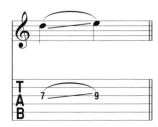

SHIFT SLIDE: Same as legato slide, except the second note is struck.

TRILL: Very rapidly alternate between the notes indicated by continuously hammering on and pulling off.

TAPPING: Hammer ("tap") the fret indicated with the pick-hand index or middle finger and pull off to the note fretted by the fret hand.

NATURAL HARMONIC: Strike the note while the fret-hand lightly touches the string directly over the fret indicated.

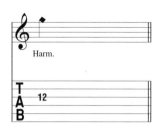

PINCH HARMONIC: The note is fretted normally and a harmonic is produced by adding the edge of the thumb or the tip of the index finger of the pick hand to the normal pick attack.

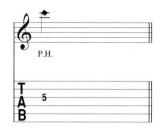

HARP HARMONIC: The note is fretted normally and a harmonic is produced by gently resting the pick hand's index finger directly above the indicated fret (in parentheses) while the pick hand's thumb or pick assists by plucking the appropriate string.

PICK SCRAPE: The edge of the pick is rubbed down (or up) the string, producing a scratchy sound.

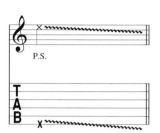

MUFFLED STRINGS: A percussive sound is produced by laying the fret hand across the string(s) without depressing, and striking them with the pick hand.

PALM MUTING: The note is partially muted by the pick hand lightly touching the string(s) just before the bridge.

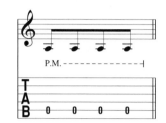

RAKE: Drag the pick across the strings indicated with a single motion.

TREMOLO PICKING: The note is picked as rapidly and continuously as possible.

ARPEGGIATE: Play the notes of the chord indicated by quickly rolling them from bottom to top.

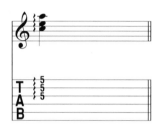

VIBRATO BAR DIVE AND RETURN: The pitch of the note or chord is dropped a specified number of steps (in rhythm), then returned to the original pitch.

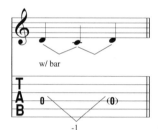

VIBRATO BAR SCOOP: Depress the bar just before striking the note, then quickly release the bar.

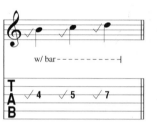

VIBRATO BAR DIP: Strike the note and then immediately drop a specified number of steps, then release back to the original pitch.

Additional Musical Definitions

(accent)	• Accentuate note (play it louder).	
(accent)	• Accentuate note with great intensity.	
(staccato)	• Play the note short.	
⊓	• Downstroke	
V	• Upstroke	

D.S. al Coda — • Go back to the sign (𝄋), then play until the measure marked "*To Coda*," then skip to the section labelled "**Coda**."

D.C. al Fine — • Go back to the beginning of the song and play until the measure marked "*Fine*" (end).

Rhy. Fig. — • Label used to recall a recurring accompaniment pattern (usually chordal).

Riff — • Label used to recall composed, melodic lines (usually single notes) which recur.

Fill — • Label used to identify a brief melodic figure which is to be inserted into the arrangement.

Rhy. Fill — • A chordal version of a Fill.

tacet — • Instrument is silent (drops out).

• Repeat measures between signs.

1. 2. — • When a repeated section has different endings, play the first ending only the first time and the second ending only the second time.

NOTE: Tablature numbers in parentheses mean:
1. The note is being sustained over a system (note in standard notation is tied), or
2. The note is sustained, but a new articulation (such as a hammer-on, pull-off, slide or vibrato) begins, or
3. The note is a barely audible "ghost" note (note in standard notation is also in parentheses).